LIAR'S CODE

LIAR'S CODE

Growing Up Fishing

RICHARD CHIAPPONE

Skyhorse Publishing

Skyhorse Publishing books may be purchased in bulk at special discounts for sales promotion, corporate gifts, fund-raising, or educational purposes. Special editions can also be created to specifications. For details, contact the Special Sales Department, Skyhorse Publishing, 307 West 36th Street, 11th Floor, New York, NY 10018 or info@skyhorsepublishing.com.

Visit our website at www.skyhorsepublishing.com.

10 9 8 7 6 5 4 3 2 1

Library of Congress Cataloging-in-Publication Data is available on file.

Cover design by Tom Lau
Cover photo credit Richard Chiappone

Print ISBN: 978-1-5107-0494-7
Ebook ISBN: 978-1-5107-0495-4

Printed in the United States of America

Go Fish

There is a boy painting a fence,
an endless white picket snake,
shedding its aging skin.

His mind drifts to the river at the end of the street,
wide and long, and thick with fish—waiting
for a boy with a rod and reel, a can of worms.

He doesn't see his mother at the clothesline,
the wooden clothespin clenched in her teeth,
can't see her aching hip, her elbow, back.

But she sees him—her firstborn—staring over the fence,
already on the water, paintbrush drying in the sun.
And she says—Richard, go on. Go ahead, honey. Go fish.

To my folks, Chip and Clara.
Every child should be so lucky.

Table of Contents

Acknowledgments

Many thanks to the editors of the following publications, where these essays appeared previously:

Anchorage Press: "Oblivious" (as "'Rich! Bear!'"), "The Killing Season," "It Takes a Thief," "The Last Fish," "The Man Who Mistook His Vacation for a Fishing Trip" (as "Southern Exposure").

The Drake: "Perfect" (as "The Feather").

Fly Rod and Reel: "Requiem for a River Bend."

Gray's Sporting Journal: "Anything But Mercy," "The Blue Pike Blues," "Egg-Sucking Everything," "Liar's Code," "The Winter Face," "Trevally Ripped Our Flesh."

MidCurrent: "Adiós, Señor Permit."

Sporting Classics: "Slamming Cuba," "This Boy's Bait."

Made of Salmon: Alaska Stories from The Salmon Project, University of Alaska Press, 2016: "The King and I."

Some were also included in *Opening Days: A Fly Fisherman Writes*, Barclay Creek Press, 2010.

And personal thanks to the friends who offered such good advice, help, and endless support for this and other projects: Jim Anker, Jim Babb, Scott Banks, Bob Bundy, Anne Coray, Pete Garay, Ann Keffer, Tom Kizzia, Mary Langham, Nancy Lord, Trish Manney, Jo-Ann Mapson, Linda Martin, Ed Murphy, Bill Rice, Zack Rogow, Judith Schnell, Teresa Sundmark, Miranda Weiss. With a special nod to Jay Cassell, whose idea this book was.

Finally, special thanks to Lin Hampson—always my first reader, always most trusted.

Introduction

The personal essays collected here were written over a period of about fifteen years and published in a half dozen journals, both regional and national. Some appeared in a previous book. In compiling them for this collection it became clear that they basically comprised a memoir in linked stories—stories from my life. Although I have also been a father, a construction worker (for nearly forty years), a working musician, a watercolor artist, a writer, and a college professor, this is an account of my life as a fisherman in three vastly different parts of the world.

The pieces are therefore organized into three groups. The first section portrays my childhood along the Niagara River, learning to fish in conditions that were less than idyllic (to say the least), and dreaming about one day moving to the Great North Woods. The second group involves reaching that goal as well as moving to Alaska in my early thirties, a huge change in scene from the industrial environs where I spent the first half of my life. The last section reflects my late-in-life, ongoing infatuation with tropical saltwater fishing, another wildly disparate environment, and about as far from both Alaska and the Rust Belt as it's possible to get.

F. Scott Fitzgerald famously said that there are no second acts in American lives. He just didn't live long enough to audition for his next role.

—Rich Chiappone, August 2015

PART I

All You Need Is Love Canal

Chapter 1

Liar's Code

BEING FISHERMEN, MY FRIENDS AND I were all great liars. We fibbed about the monster perch caught in the Niagara River at the end of our street when none of the other kids were around. We jacked up the number of bullheads or sunnies hauled in on family vacations, far from the neighborhood. Fish that got away ballooned with each telling, like the river's algae blooms in August. All honest "stretchers," as Huck would have it. And we never called each other on them. We never would.

Deceit is in my blood. My grandfather once told me about being a young man in Sicily, playing cards with his friends. "Everybody knew everybody at the table was cheating," he said. Then he paused, as grandfathers will when dispensing wisdom. "But nobody said anything!" He smiled at the memory and added, nostalgically, "Of course everybody had a knife."

In our neighborhood, the liar's code worked the same way, except without the weapons. And, really, who was hurt by our endless fish tales?

Then came ninth grade, when Catholic boys were seined from every junior high in the city to attend Bishop Duffy High School, and all rules were off. There I met Kelleher, who was from a different world, and a different class of liars altogether.

Kelleher and I were the two smallest boys in a school known for its gigantic football goons of Irish, Italian, and Polish extraction. Those monsters bounced us off the walls like mice in a cattle car, used us for target practice in dodgeball, swung us on the gym-class ropes like pet monkeys. Too small to go out for any team, we nursed our wounds at the bus stop after school, while the varsity gorillas stayed late stomping school spirit into each other in the practice-field mud. When Kelleher and I discovered our shared love of fishing, the stories began.

Kelleher had the weary face of an old man, with eyes set darkly in deep sockets and further shadowed by a hint of pained experience a kid our age shouldn't have known; somehow this gave his every story credibility. He lived in the inner city, far from the river, and shouldn't have known a thing about fishing, but his father owned a cabin in the Allegheny Mountains, south of Buffalo, which, compared to my home waters, the fetid industrial Niagara, was like owning a boat on the River Spey or a floatplane in Alaska.

He told me about a huge brown trout lurking in the unnamed creek on their property, a fish so old and wise it wouldn't take a hooked live sculpin in the middle of the night, though it had once made a move on a Mepps Spinner he'd offered.

"I could see halfway down its throat," he said as we waited for his bus. Kelleher made a circle with both thumbs and forefingers to show me the size of the trout's mouth. "That fish'll go eight pounds, easy." The manic barks of the football coach and the pained grunts of clashing linemen hung in the damp September air. Kelleher's bus pulled up.

"So what happened?" I asked, as he shouldered his book bag and took out his token.

"Struck too fast. Reflexes. Yanked the spinner right out of its mouth and snagged in the roots. You'll see it hanging there if you come with us this weekend."

"Will that be all right with your dad?"

I'd never met anyone with a cabin, and didn't know if people routinely invited strangers to their retreats.

"Oh yeah," he said. "I bring guys with us all the time."

He stepped up into his bus, took a seat, and hung out the window. "I bet that hog would go for a small Flatfish," he said. "Frog pattern."

"Maybe a Rapala!" I shouted over the roar of the bus.

But he'd already pulled his head inside, and my words were lost in a cloud of exhaust. From the football field, Coach Melvoy howled, "*Defense!*"

* * *

Tuesday, I saw Kelleher between second and third period. He told me that, in the slower water, you couldn't keep the smallmouths off a black Mister Twister. "Seventeen inches, some of them," he said. "You're going to love this creek."

"My folks aren't too sure," I said. "They want to know what time we'll be back."

"Sunday late. My father and I like to make a full weekend of it. That's the way we are down there in the woods. Late Sunday, tell them. Very late."

A full weekend at a cabin in the wild Southern Tier sounded great to me. Most weekends my father played accordion at weddings; I don't think he'd ever been south of Cheektowaga in his life. Fish were something he brought home from Felice's on meatless Fridays—breaded and fried, with coleslaw.

"How many bass have you caught?" I asked Kelleher as the bell rang and a stampede of enormous men dressed as boys blundered around us.

"How many?" Kelleher repeated. He trained those weary, hooded eyes on me and nodded like an old sailor giving up a treasured detail of an epic voyage. "More than you can shake a stick at."

He slammed his locker shut and hurried down the now empty hall, and I stood there. *More than you can shake a stick at.* It sounded like something my grandfather would say. But all I really heard was, *bass, trout, mountains, cabin, bass, trout, mountains.*

Father Moretti gave me detention for being late to class. I used the time to make a list of things I'd need at the cabin.

* * *

Wednesday in the cafeteria, over Spanish rice and gray string beans, Kelleher casually mentioned that we could always catch "a mess" of native brookies. "If we want to bother with them."

The only brook trout I'd ever seen were either on a Winslow Homer calendar down at the Mobil Station, or lying on a bed of fresh-plucked ferns in a Genesee Cream Ale ad. Kelleher said "hundreds" of them lived in the feeder streams that flowed into the creek by his cabin. "They don't get big. Twelve inches, maybe." He forked a heap of Spanish rice into his mouth. Around it, he added, "Fourteen, tops."

A fourteen-inch brook trout.

"Can your father call mine?" I asked.

His face went dark. He stopped chewing. "What about?"

"You know, that it's okay for me to go with you and sleep over and all."

"Look," Kelleher said, "I don't see him every day. I live with my mother."

I felt my face flush.

"I just mean . . . well, my parents will want to talk to—"

"I don't like to bug him," he said. "We'll pick you up Saturday morning, seven-thirty. They can meet him then. Good enough?"

He went back to eating, silent and more serious than I'd ever seen him.

"The brookies," I said. "What do they hit? I mean, if we bother with them?"

"Anything." He was smiling again. "Everyone knows they're the easiest trout to fool."

* * *

By Thursday I was missing questions even the football goons answered, failing tests I could've written. When I wasn't staring out the classroom window at the smokestack of the graphite plant where my father worked, imagining that cabin in the hills, I was making lists of lures and baits to bring: salted minnows, nightcrawlers, and wood grubs for the trout; spinners, jigs, and soft-shell crayfish for the bass. I fasted like a monk, saving my lunch money all week. After school I went to Cruickshank's Tackle Shop and bought split-shot, snelled hooks, and a small Daredevil spoon to fool that monster brown.

"You might bring a couple of big plugs," Kelleher said as he looked over my list. "Pikie Minnows, maybe."

I looked at him. "Pikie Minnows?"

"I was reeling in a small trout one time and something huge nearly tore it in half. Muskie, I figured from the bite radius."

The bite radius? "A muskie? In the mountains?" I said.

"Hey, who knows? Chautauqua Lake isn't that far away. Maybe an osprey or a kingfisher picked up a small one and dropped it in the creek. Wouldn't take long to grow big with all the food in there."

A muskie. It sounded perfectly reasonable to me.

* * *

If I attended classes that Friday I have no memory of it. I vaguely recall staggering through the halls, shoved and hip-checked from one giant to the next, and not caring. At lunch I got Kelleher to look at the schedule I'd worked out. We'd fish for bass when we got to the cabin Saturday morning, maybe cast some big lures for that muskie. Midday we'd go for the brookies in the feeder streams, and wait until evening for that old brown. We'd leave Sunday flexible, so we could fill our limits of each species, on the odd chance we hadn't already. I'd drawn it all up on a chart.

"Looks good to me," Kelleher said. Then, as if it had just occurred to him, he said, "I don't know if you're interested, but when we're up this one feeder creek, remind me to show you a pool where I had something odd-looking rise to a Black Gnat one time."

"Odd-looking?"

"Don't get your hopes up, but have you ever heard of grayling?"

Obviously, I should have screamed, "*Grayling?* In New York State?" But by then if Kelleher had said, "giant squid," I would've gone shopping for a harpoon.

That night, while the rest of the student body cheered and stamped their feet like buffalo in the football stands, I packed a lunch for the ride down to the mountains, spread all my tackle across the kitchen table, honed hooks, oiled my spinning reel, practiced tying barrel knots, and polished every piece of metal on every spinner and spoon I owned. I made myself a bed on the couch in the living room so the early-morning alarm wouldn't disturb my parents and little brothers and sisters. All night I lay there staring at the ceiling, trying to picture the mountains, the cabin, the creek.

Saturday morning, as the sun rose, my gear sat heaped on the curb and I paced the sidewalk in front of our house, my brain alternating between disappointment and hatred. I kicked our fence so hard I broke a slat, screamed at God Himself in the heavens above, and later went to confession. I spent that evening down at the river, smashing bottles against the bridge abutments, too angry even to fish. Maybe too angry ever to fish again.

* * *

Monday morning, oblivious to the triumphant jocks and their fans rampaging up and down the hall, I caught Kelleher in front of homeroom. I planned to punch him—first thing—and I didn't care if Father Moretti excommunicated me, a kind of eternal detention. I wanted to maim Kelleher, to *kill* him. It was all I'd thought about for two days. Yet when I faced him, I found myself talking instead. Or maybe whining.

"I waited all morning."

"Sorry," he said. "Something came up."

"I set the alarm for five o'clock so I could catch more night-crawlers before it got light."

"Hey, that's a good idea," he said. "Really. I'll remember that one."

"Sat on the curb like a jerk. My sisters are still laughing! My brothers."

"Oh, man, that bites," he said. "I don't have any brothers or sisters, thank God."

"What happened?" I hoped there was a truly good reason for the betrayal.

He told me there'd been a mix-up. That his father'd invited some men for the weekend. He didn't know my last name, couldn't call me. It occurred to me that I didn't know his first name, but I was too pissed to think about that.

"I tried to call you," I said. "There are no Kellehers in the phone book."

"Um, it's under my mother's last name. And my father lives in Tonawanda. Sorry."

My anger sagged. I'd kept it afloat as long as I could. "So your father went with his friends. Does that mean you didn't go either?" The thought made me feel better.

"Oh, I went. Me and my dad and two guys he works with at the GM plant."

"You went?" I was ready for the bullshit fish story. What would it be—sea-run salmon? Land-locked stripers? I was ready to nail him.

"We didn't fish much," he said. "Mostly we spent the weekend scouting for grouse."

"Grouse?"

"And woodcock."

He told me about the feral apple orchards the grouse loved, the great bottomland woodcock cover, while all around us jersey-wearing giants traded high-fives, lockers slammed shut, and students pushed on to homeroom.

"Woodcock," I muttered.

"Neighbors have a cornfield, too, where we can get some pheasants—you know, when we've limited out on grouse and timberdoodles. You should come, opening day. No, you're *definitely* coming. I'll talk to my dad about it."

Kelleher went on and on until the bell rang, and, trained as I was to respond to the stimulus, I drifted toward homeroom, his last words hanging in the air—*turkeys, birdshot, modified choke . . .*

I took my seat. A brute named Farnucci leaned over from the next desk to stab me in the ribs with a thick forefinger. But he couldn't reach me. I was already halfway to the mountains.

Chapter 2

The Blue Pike Blues

THE WORLD IS FILLED WITH two kinds of people. There are those who live in the vividly real present, embrace the possibilities of the future, and know precisely where the past belongs (i.e., in the past). And then there are those of us who fish.

With the possible exception of teachers of Romantic Poetry, we fishermen are the biggest bunch of dewey-eyed nostalgics on earth. Never mind that even the fairly recent past was a time of outdoor toilets, unrefrigerated beer, and death by impacted wisdom teeth—not to mention serious hardships like untapered fly lines and those cast iron Herter's fly-tying vises that smashed hooks into tiny molecules of steel rubble. To a fisherman, the only thing that matters about the cold, uncomfortable, disease-ridden past is that the fishing was better—much, much better by nearly all accounts. That's why the first full sentence a young angler learns to say is "It sure ain't what it used to be."

AS A KID IN THE late 1950s and early '60s, I lived on the banks of the Upper Niagara River, a few miles above the famous falls and just downstream from the infamous Love Canal. There I spent some of the happiest days of my life in the shadows of the tanks and towers of the Hooker Chemical, Union Carbide, and DuPont plants, wading up to my hips and diligently casting into the fetid, rainbow-hued waters, catching almost nothing, ever, and listening to the older men bemoaning how bad things were and how much better they used to be.

My own father didn't fish much, working days at the graphite plant and weekends playing his accordion at weddings to keep me and my numerous younger brothers and sisters in sneakers and pimple creams. So I would go next door on summer evenings and sit on the porch with my best friend, Danny Humic (an only child), and listen to his father tell stories of the incredible fishing he'd had as a young man just after World War II. Apparently, in those misty days before my time, the Niagara was still vital and fecund enough to withstand the onslaught of the heavy industry that had been lured there to its banks by cheap hydroelectricity. The stories about the fishing abounded.

For example, in the Lower Niagara where it flows into Lake Ontario, there were once so many blue pike (a small subspecies of walleye), that two men in a wooden skiff, drift fishing with their hexagonal steel casting rods (this was pre-fiberglass) and those old backlash prone casting reels they used to use (this was also pre-spinning), could catch dozens, if not hundreds, of the tasty little pikeperch in an afternoon, feed their families, and sell the rest of their fish to the neighborhood saloons where the sweet white fillets appeared on the menu several days a week.

Not only were there more of every species in those halcyon days, the stories went, but everything was gargantuan. Mr. Humic had a photo of himself as a young boy in the 1930s straddling the enormous midsection of a ten-foot sturgeon his uncle had caught on a trotline in the Niagara just off the end of the street where we lived. A few miles upriver, within sight of the Lackawanna steel mills, anglers trolling with Pikie Minnow plugs took some of the biggest muskies in North America. And, almost directly under the falls, in the foamy eddies near the Maid of the Mist tour boat dock, Mr. Humic himself (the first fly fisherman I ever met) used to catch stringers of hefty smallmouth bass using a wooden popper with bucktail legs. I got to see the actual lure, its frog-spotted paint job nearly lost to the teeth of fish I could only imagine, as Mr. Humic reverently lifted the relic from his tackle box as though it were the jawbone of the great fisherman, St. Peter himself.

I fished nearly every weekend under Mr. Humic's generous tutelage, from when I was ten years old to when I turned eighteen and I realized that it was 1967 and time to grow a beard and learn to play a guitar. And between Danny, his father, and myself, we might have caught two dozen game fish of any kind in all those years. It seemed as though there had been this brief moment when the victorious GIs returned from Europe and the South Pacific and were rewarded not only with a robust economy and decent paying jobs, but with American rivers and lakes still teeming with fish. Danny Humic and I and the rest of that huge new bubble of postwar babies grew into fishermen just as the fish disappeared. By the mid-1960s, a good day on the Niagara was one with a couple of rock bass in it.

On weekdays during the summer, Danny and I would fish for bullheads, chubs, eels, sunfish, suckers, and the dull-eyed freshwater drum we called sheephead. Many a day we were thankful for a few stunted white bass—which would hit a spinner and obviate the need to drown worms. We read every article in every magazine and we tried every lure that we could scrape up the money to buy: Mepps, Abu Reflex, Lazy Ike, Swimmerspoon, River Runt, you name it. We shoveled sidewalks in the snowy Western New York winters and bought modern, pushbutton, closed-face spinning reels that allowed us to cast out far beyond the oil-glossed shallows and into what we believed was the oh-so-fishy deep. Evenings, I read books about trout, and taught myself to tie flies—hoping that one day I might get to see a stream that held those magical, speckled, and rainbow-sided creatures. Sometimes I would go down to the Niagara at the end of the street and use my fiberglass Sears fly rod to practice casting and watch my flies float on the surface and pretend to believe that somehow there might, for some reason, be a remnant trout or a salmon left living there in those oil-slicked waters just waiting for a chance to rise up and slurp down my ragged offering.

The Niagara was gagging on broken bottles and drowned metal drums, tires, wheels, complete cars and astounding quantities of building materials: roofing shingles, red tile pipe, lengths of rusting rebar, and massive chunks of ragged concrete. It was as though a ruined civilization had been plowed into the water at the end of my street.

And then there was the algae. The algae that feasted on the yet-to-be-outlawed phosphates in the soap flakes our industrious mothers used to scrub our muddy, bait-stained clothes. The algae that smothered the underwater rocks and trash, growing and blooming until it became so dense it broke free in undulating globs that made it impossible to cast into the river without pulling up slimy green ropes of what looked like overcooked Swiss chard.

But it was even sicker than it appeared, poisoned by chemicals we couldn't see: dioxins, PCBs, mirex, and the deadly heavy metals that settled into the silted bottom, where they would lie mixed into the organic matter the smallest invertebrates ate, contaminating the food chain from the bottom up.

Everywhere Danny and I went—at the last remaining bait shop, or down at the nearly empty marinas—grown men would glance at the fishing rods strapped to our bikes, turn their eyes away from the stunted bullheads on the stringer dangling from the handlebars, and shake their weary heads, muttering something about blue pike.

The first rule of plumbing is that everything disgusting runs downhill, and we were downhill from Illinois, Michigan, and Ohio (where you could roast marshmallows at the Cuyahoga River without bringing any matches). Only Lake Ontario, fifteen miles downstream from us, was in worse shape. Lake Ontario was a virtual inland ocean with 7,340 square miles of surface, millions of gallons of water pouring down over the great falls and through the Lower Niagara into it every day, and carrying with it every foul thing that the not so great lakes, Superior, Michigan, Huron, and Erie had flushed out.

Please, don't get me wrong; I'm not complaining. Really, I'm not.

Unlike poor Mr. Humic, Danny's father, who had seen the glorious full-stringered days of the '40s and '50s, I had nothing to compare our dismal fishing with, and enjoyed what I assumed was a wonderful time, blithely slipping and sliding over algae-covered industrial waste in pursuit of trash fish. To this very day, I thank God I had the opportunity to grow up on the banks of a river (such as it was) instead of on a farm, say, or a country club, where less fortunate boys have been known to take up kicking inflated pigskins or clubbing little white balls into holes in the ground.

Moreover, having been confirmed a fisherman in the Church of the Perpetually Skunked I was prepared for challenging angling later in life—saltwater fishing, for instance. Some of my current flats fishing partners grew up in places where people actually caught fish, and they suffer mightily at the cruelty of uncooperative permit, finicky tarpon, and over-nervous bonefish—all of which, on any given day, I am fully prepared to not catch.

I'm simply not qualified to say, "It ain't as good as it used to be," because as near as I can tell things have never been better.

Consider this. In the 1970s, finally driven out of Western New York by an economy even worse than its fishing, I moved west and kept going until I hit Alaska, where I have lived for the past three decades. Alaska's fishing is superb by any standards, but for a kid from the Love Canal it has been nothing short of dreamlike. So I never bothered to look back. Last November, however, I was in Niagara County to visit family and I wandered down to Eighteen Mile Creek near Burt, NY, a few miles from my brother Mike's house, to get a little perspective.

The streams there along the shore of Lake Ontario are mere trickles, environments suited more for the pumpkinseeds and rock bass I once fished for. So, as I walked from the parking lot down the newly paved path to Eighteen Mile Creek, I was curious about rumors of fall-run trout stocked in the lake and fattened on the baitfish smorgasbord there. Halfway down the path, a man in camouflage waders came struggling up, hauling behind him a stringer of enormous brown trout. The thirty or forty pounds of dead trout attached to his rope were being thoroughly scaled and more or less eviscerated by the rough new asphalt over which they were being dragged. That was a first for me. When I was a kid, trout were as foreign and exotic as belly dancers—and at least as desirable.

There was a wire mesh trash can, conveniently placed at the bottom of the path to the water; it was loaded with fish. Up and down at the creek the madness continued. Dozens of five- to ten-pound browns and a few steelhead lay strewn among the dead autumn leaves. Everywhere, anglers cast bobbers and bait, apparently determined to catch and kill these giant trout and throw them away. Someone explained that all they wanted from the fish was the roe, which they would then use for bait to catch more trout—I guess, to get more eggs to catch more trout. And so on. Or something. I was so stunned by the mayhem, I'm sure I didn't get it straight.

It is true that those eggs won't survive in the warm, sluggish creeks, and that eating the flesh of Lake Ontario fish is discouraged due to residual PCBs and other heavy poisons dumped into the Niagara back when I was wading there fifty years ago. But having once been reduced to fishing for eels, I'm still not sure what to make of seeing guys so ardently trashing trout. It's like trying to figure out which is worse: a Muzak rendition of an already painful Barry Manilow tune or their interpretation of "Ruby Tuesday." A tough call, for sure.

One thing certain is that Niagara County has changed. The once moribund Lower Niagara gets written up today in sporting magazines touting its spectacular steelhead fishing, huge schools of lake trout fin in the deep eddies below the hydro dam, and charter captains troll for salmon and trout in a lake where smelt once ruled the waves.

Change is rarely completely good or bad. The Clean Water Act(s) of 1972 and 1977 obviously made a difference in the Great Lakes. Divers will tell you that in the now clear water they can see sturgeon feeding again at the mouth of the Niagara beneath the two-hundred-year-old cannons of historic Fort Niagara. Sure, the water is clear, in part, because of the billions of non-native zebra mussels that have swarmed the Great Lakes, so these new sport fishing opportunities are available in somewhat less than Edenic conditions. Today Lake Ontario is clear enough to see the bottom, though not the carcinogens that coat it. The creeks are full of trout, but the trout have little value now. On the other hand, while the blue pike may be lost forever, my young nephews and grandsons don't have to fish for chubs.

I think my brother Mike displays a healthy pragmatic spirit when he says, "It's great! Now you can see a beer can fifty feet down."

Exactly.

Chapter 3

This Boy's Bait

THE FIRST TIME I SAW the Presti brothers, they were sprinkling coffee grounds across the front lawn of the little GI Bill house my family had just moved into, one block inland from the Niagara River. It was 1953, and the youngest Presti, Cosmo, and I would start kindergarten together at Pacific Avenue Elementary in a few days.

Neither five-year-old Cosmo nor I had yet contracted the uncontrollable obsession with catching fish that still plagues me today. But his older brothers, already afflicted with that madness, had been feeding and harvesting nightcrawlers from the front lawn of the house I just moved into for years. What the Presti brothers knew, and what I learned eventually, was that, with a level-wind bait-casting rig, a half-ounce bell sinker, a package of snelled hooks, and a can of fresh-picked worms, a boy could catch almost everything that swam in the Niagara. Cosmo and I came down with the fever soon enough. And since the only treatment (and not much of a cure) for the fishing disease is fishing itself, we picked worms most summer nights for the next ten years.

It's probably safe to say that the common earthworm—our "nightcrawlers" being the fattest, thickest, and longest North

American member of the Annelida phylum—is the "gateway" substance that ushers most young boys into the addiction we call angling. Like millions of young fishermen before us, Cosmo and I caught our first fish, stoneroller chubs, on half a worm.

All summer long, throughout our grade school years, our lawns looked like rice paddies as we let the garden hose run and run until our parents screamed at us. Evenings, after the last hide-and-seek games fizzled out, and the faint blue glow of *What's My Line?* or *Bonanza* emanated from living room windows, we crept on hands and knees across the soggy grass, flashlight beams dancing before us as we tugged stretchy nightcrawlers from their holes. We suffered wet knees, mosquito bites, fingers punctured by thorny red barberry clippings, and, less painful but far worse, surprise handfuls of undetected dog droppings. But we got bait.

Neither Cosmo's father nor mine fished, and so our fishing was limited to places along the river we could reach on foot or bicycle. That meant behind the cement docks, behind the water plant, behind Hooker Chemical Co. This was nearly two decades before the Clean Water Act; the city of Niagara Falls is downstream from the steel mills of Buffalo, the automakers of Detroit, the stockyards of Chicago, and the timber yards and iron ore docks of Thunder Bay, Duluth, and Sault St. Marie. Most days, if we caught anything, we caught chubs, carp, a stunted white bass or two, and we went fishless altogether on many. If angling were a team sport, our mascot would have been a skunk.

For much of the 1950s, gathering bait was almost always more satisfying than fishing with it. Then the summer after fifth grade, a small, two-bedroom home, a lot like mine, sprang up on the vacant lot next door. At first I mourned the loss of my secret hiding places in the sticky milkweeds, the garter snakes and toads I caught there, the Christmas tree forts and snow forts and clubhouses made of scrounged building supplies my pals and I would no longer be constructing. But when a boy my own age, Danny Humic, moved into the new house, everything changed for me. Danny's father was a serious fisherman. They owned a boat. A boat! I wouldn't have been more excited if a troupe of female nudists had set up camp there.

This came at an opportune time. Cosmo Presti, my staunch fishing pal since kindergarten, was impossibly handsome—even as a small child. In our first grade class picture, he stares out at the camera, his hair combed back in a ducktail pompadour, an impatient irritation on his face, as if he'd been called away from cocktails with a beautiful woman to have his picture taken with us children. You could pencil a black moustache under his six-year-old nose, and it would look perfectly normal there. The rest of us look like freshly scrubbed potatoes. By the time sixth grade rolled around, not only had he discovered girls in earnest, they'd discovered him. To my great disappointment, Cosmo set his fishing rod aside, began wearing ironed shorts, and started practicing the Twist. Far too shy to dance with (or even talk to) girls, I found myself in need of a new best friend.

Enter Danny Humic. Danny was an only child, and Mr. Humic was happy to bring me along on their fishing trips—probably in part to distract the chatty Danny and get a few minutes' peace and quiet. My house was filling up with younger siblings (I am the oldest of seven), and I was equally happy to join the two Humic men on their trips. The Humics' boat—a ten-foot Grumman aluminum skiff with a seven-and-a-half horsepower Mercury outboard—fit on top of their Ford Fairlane station wagon. For the next five years or so, we took it out almost every summer weekend, fishing the upper Niagara from the Peace Bridge at Fort Erie downstream to the treacherous Navy Island drifts, just a couple short miles above the deadly falls. When we really felt adventurous, we car-topped the skiff up into Ontario, north of Toronto, where we camped, and fished Georgian Bay, Lake Simcoe, and the Kawartha Lakes.

My baitfishing horizons expanded. Winters, we jigged through thick Lake Erie ice for perch and smelt, impaling the larvae from goldenrod galls on our bright chrome hooks. Right after ice-out in the spring, we fished small shiner minnows for fat bullheads in Jordan Harbor off Lake Ontario. Summers on the Niagara, we drifted for black bass with chubs, carefully threaded through the lips, learning to resist the urge to set the hook on the first bite, instead opening the bails on our new Garcia Mitchell 300 spinning reels and feeding out line until the bass had turned the bait in their mouths. We caught grasshoppers and crickets and fished them on fine wire hooks for wild brook trout in small clear streams up on the Bruce Peninsula. We fished for monster spring run rainbows in the Finger Lakes streams using huge white wood grubs with frightening pincers. And yes, we fished with worms too. Danny's father expropriated the insulated aluminum milk box in which the Wendt's Dairy delivery man left his bottles by the Humic side door. We never went anywhere without it—full of peat moss and nightcrawlers.

* * *

I've lived in Alaska now for more than thirty years, where live bait is prohibited by fish and game regulations to limit the invasion of non-native species. I haven't impaled anything alive on a hook for decades, and one of the things I miss about bait fishing is the wonderful variety of predator fish that live bait attracted—including species you'll rarely catch on a lure or a fly. Eels, for example, provided us endless hours of entertainment, as well as various members of the catfish family, yellow suckers, and, of course, carp. I realize that carp have now been declared respectable fly rod fish, and that there are carp fly patterns, carp guides, probably a line of carp fishing apparel and sunglasses. Fine. I don't doubt the difficulty of fooling them, their selectiveness, or their fighting capabilities. I just cannot erase my memories of the first couple decades of my life spent spearing, shooting, or otherwise disrespecting them. But the hardest thing to forget is their fetid environs, and the way they spent their days rooting through the industrial wastewaters of my youth. Though, now that I've written that, I have to admit I spent a lot of said youth doing exactly that myself.

While I'm thinking about the sometimes ugly fish drawn to bait, this comes to mind: The summer between sixth and seventh grades, I went camping for a whole week with Danny Humic and his mother and father on the Pickerel River up in Canada. Hundreds of miles north of our hometown, we parked the Humic Ford in a lot next to a tackle shop, where the highway crossed the river. We launched the little skiff, piled high with the four of us and a week's worth of camping gear, and very little freeboard. This was way before lightweight Gore-Tex and graphite gear—I'm talking an Army surplus canvas tent that looked like it might belong to Barnum and Bailey, a Coleman stove, cans of Spam and Dinty Moore stew, gas cans for the outboard, tackle boxes that weighed nearly as much as I did at that time. It was more expedition than camping trip. We motored a few miles up the slow moving river and found a huge slab of Precambrian bedrock sloping down to the water, hauled the gear to the aromatic pine forest at the top, pitched camp, and went fishing.

Using spinners draped with juicy nightcrawlers, we caught smallmouths, rock bass, and the most desirable food fish of the region: walleyes, which the Canadians call yellow pickerel—the eponymous pickerel of that river. But to catch the northern pike that haunted the weedy bays bookending the giant slab of rock, we needed a serious mouthful of live bait. So Mr. Humic would take his bamboo fly rod (the first one I'd ever seen) and a dry fly and catch baby perch off the rocky shore.

Danny and I would hook the unlucky perch just under the dorsal fin on heavy, straight-eyed hooks, three feet below red and white plastic bobbers the size of baseballs. Casting the rigs out to the edge of the lily pads, we'd prop our rods in forked sticks—as has been the tradition of bait fishermen since time immemorial—with the bails open on the reels so that the rigs did not get dragged into the river, and leave the crippled perch to their fates. Then we got busy building unneeded campfires, pointlessly throwing rocks into the river, or shooting bullfrogs with Danny's Crosman pellet rifle. When one of the bobbers started cruising along upstream against the current, one of us would usually haul in a typical hammer-handle northern. The small pike were savage and hyperkinetic—for about one minute—and then generally came in docilely.

But one day Danny's bobber disappeared altogether, and when he reared back on his rod, something strong took off into the depths of the river, the reel screaming as line played out. We briefly hoped Danny's leviathan would turn out to be a truly gigantic northern, or maybe even a musky. What finally came to the bank however was be a huge bowfin, over two feet long. The bowfin—we called them dogfish—is a Jurassic-era lungfish, and looks every bit as primitive as its two-hundred-million-year history would suggest. Later that week, a much larger bowfin plowed through the wall of the little rock corral we kept our walleyes alive in—we had no refrigeration for a week in the warm Ontario summer weather—effecting a prison break of sorts; we managed to chase the prehistoric monster off and repair the wall, only losing a few fish. And then, a few days later as we drifted the river, another even larger specimen rose from the green murk alongside the boat and inhaled a fifteen-inch walleye right off the chain stringer. After that, Danny and I found all manner of reasons to cancel our afternoon swims.

But the bait I remember most vividly when I think of that time in my life were the live frogs we used to fish for walleyes in the Kawartha Lakes in the mid-1960s. It was a happy time in my childhood, and the names of those lakes pierce me like a laser of sentimentality—Buckhorn Lake, Pigeon Lake, Rice Lake—leaving me aching with romantic longing in a way none of my high school girlfriends' names do. Obviously being more nostalgic about weedy

Canadian lakes I fished fifty years ago than the girls I once loved says something about me, but I don't really want to know what.

When Danny's father heard through the local fishing grapevine that the walleyes in the Kawarthas were fools for live frogs, Danny and I hung his minnow bucket off the handlebars of his bike, lashed a long-handled net to the cross bar of mine, and pedaled across the massive Grand Island Bridge to Buckhorn State Park, an undeveloped tract of swampland and cattails occupying the north end of the big island in the middle of the Niagara River.

It was June, and the resident leopard and pickerel frogs had just absorbed their tadpole tails and sprouted legs. They were an inch or two long, the perfect size to be bait. We caught dozens of them. That Friday, when Danny's father came home from his job at Alox Chemicals, we threw the aluminum skiff on the car-top and drove up into Canada, the frogs hopping madly about in the minnow bucket, making a racket like a drum solo. This was forty years before the 9/11 attacks changed everything; the border guards didn't even lift the little trap door on top and look inside.

Fishing with live frogs is not for the faint at heart. I must say I would not even consider it now, at my age, close enough to death myself to resist inflicting a gruesome demise on anything smaller and weaker than me. If that sounds a little prissy, sue me. I guess with age instead of wisdom, I got squeamish empathy.

But at fourteen, with just the vaguest concept of mortality whispering for attention in a brain clogged with either fishing or sex fantasies, I drifted on the breeze across the Kawartha Lakes in the Humics' little aluminum skiff with a live frog hooked through the chin, a couple split shot on the line to sink it to fishy levels. Just as we did when fishing with large chubs for bass, we would open the bail of our reels when a walleye bit on a frog, waiting—more or less patiently—for the predator to swallow its prey.

However, being fourteen years old, patience was a quality neither Danny nor I possessed in abundance, and we often struck too soon. If you have ever seen the toothy maw of a walleye—a cavern, lined with needle-sharp stalactites—you can imagine what a prematurely jerked frog might look like. Often, only the head would remain on the hook, severed from the body with the precision you see when a shark cuts a hooked bonefish in half. And *that* was a relatively merciful way for a frog to depart this life. Sometimes, only the hind legs were snipped off. Sometimes, a frog would return to the boat, more or less intact, but with its spotted skin dangling inside-out from the toes of its webbed feet. I hate to admit that none of this bothered me at the time. In retrospect, I feel less guilty when I consider the relatively minor cruelty of frog abuse against the larger backdrop of the mayhem and violence we lived with in the 1960s. Still, if I get to the Pearly Gates and find a large spotted amphibian in charge, I'll know I'm in trouble.

I think I quit fishing with frogs the day I hooked one on my line and made a forceful cast into Burnt Ship Creek, under the NY State Thruway bridge there, an old stone structure built in the 1930s. I was using a newfangled Zebco pushbutton reel, unaware that—without the drag of the spool on my old level wind—the velocity of each cast had increased exponentially. The hooked frog hit the cobblestone face of the bridge going about the speed of the Thruway traffic overhead. Realistically, I suppose that was a lot kinder death than it faced among the pike I hoped to catch with it. But whenever I go back East to visit family and drive over that little stone bridge, I can hear that terrible froggy *smack* still echoing across the lily pads.

Of course, some animals are simply cuter and therefore harder to brutalize than others. In a small tackle shop somewhere up in Canada, Danny Humic and I puzzled aloud over a display of fine wire harnesses with big treble hooks dangling off them. The owner explained ruefully that they weren't for sale, because, "nowadays, people don't like to see you fishing for northerns with live ducklings." No, I suppose they didn't—even in those days.

Fishing is a blood sport. Anyone who says differently is kidding himself. And yet, so many of us set aside our childish bait-fishing ways to take up the high-ground precepts of catch and release fly fishing, and actually try to deny that harsh truth. It was Keats who coined the term "negative capability," which he described as being able to hold two contrary ideas in your mind without going batty. It's a handy facility for a fisherman here in Alaska. For the past thirty years, I've been able to take up fly fishing, mostly for trout, with all its attendant high moral poses, yet happily continue to use frozen herring to kill salmon and halibut, and eat them. That means I never really forget that catch-and-release fishing is the cruelest sport of all. Without the excuse of feeding ourselves, there is really no explaining why we do what we do to fish. "Torment and release" would be closer to the truth. Still, I'm not hanging up the fly rod any time soon. That's one more thing I hope I never have to explain to any higher power.

Living in Alaska, my freshwater fishing is done exclusively with flies now. But out there on the briny deep of Cook Inlet, a few hundred yards from my house, all rules are off. Sometimes it's just a matter of physics; it would be mighty hard to get a fly down to halibut, rockfish, or lingcod in one hundred fifty feet of water with the tide running. We either tie on a two-pound sinker and stab a chunk of herring onto a circle hook, or lower a lead-head jig the size of a respectable trout down to them. We troll all winter for kings, using downriggers, flasher-dodgers and small herring, the leader threaded through the vent and out the mouth, using a long needle. That would obviously be painful for the herring, if they were not already dead, conveniently killed by the good folks at the Alaska Bait Co. It is nice to have someone else doing the dirty work. But forget all the squishy, squeamish modern concerns about just how murderous it's okay to be. Let's face it: Clubbing a sea-bright salmon to death and cutting its gills to bleed it out is pretty exciting.

And you never know when your mannered fly-fishing ways will intersect with the bloody exigencies of meat hunting. The summer of 1994, I was working on the construction of a new school in the remote Alaska Peninsula village of Chignik Bay. The cannery there processed the local sockeye harvest and discharged the offal from all those gutted salmon into the bay. That attracted halibut, a species generally beyond the reach of shore-bound anglers. Here, the big flatfish came right up to the rocky shoreline.

I hadn't brought any meat-fishing tackle with me; I thought I would find rainbow trout or char in the local streams that the salmon ran up. So, I brought my first graphite fly rod, a five-weight "light line series" from Sage, an expensive gift from my wife. Alas, there was no fishable freshwater near the remote job site.

I discovered, however, that some of the carpenters and sheet-rockers had been catching halibut off a rocky point jutting into the bay—although nobody had a rod or reel. Following their instructions, I took a hundred feet of heavy white construction string (used for laying out foundations, etc.), tied on one of the massive steel nuts used to bolt down the structural steel beams that supported the building, and then a circle hook purchased at the Chignik village store. I begged a few scraps of salmon trimmings from the back door of the cannery and walked to the rocks. I brought my fly rod too. I'm not sure why.

As instructed, I baited the hook and whirled the business end of the rig over my head like a lasso, and let it fly. I was standing on the line, and it jerked back, sending the bait flying off the hook. Astonished, I watched a huge halibut cruise into the shallows and gobble it. I managed to talk myself out of a heart attack, re-baited, and cast a second time. This one landed in a kelp bed to my right, and by the time I yanked it loose, the bait was gone once more. I had one decent piece of salmon belly left. The third cast was good. But when the bite came, transmitted directly through the line to my hand, I yanked back—forgetting everything I'd learned about fishing with frogs and chubs, thirty years prior, and jerking the hook out of the halibut's mouth. I was out of bait.

So, I rigged the fly rod, tied a wooly bugger on the tippet, and cast out along the edge of the weeds. I soon had a small, colorful Pacific greenling in hand. I cut it into pieces, and set the fly rod aside. Fully aware of the ironies involved with using a graphite fly rod to catch bait for a handline, I cast the heavy steel bolt and baited circle hook out into the bay once more.

In retrospect, I realize that a better fisherman could have certainly caught those halibut on a sink tip and some kind of flashy, fishy-looking streamer. Still, of all the memorable fish I've caught on flies—from a big Henry's Fork rainbow I fooled with a size 20 pheasant tail nymph, a ten-pound Bahamian bonefish caught on a Kaufman's shrimp pattern, and a nearly twenty-pound Gulf of Alaska silver salmon caught on a bunch of orange marabou lashed to a Gamakatsu hook—I have to say, landing a five-pound "chicken" halibut off those rocks, using carpenter string and a gob of greenling guts, remains, to this day, one of the most exciting moments in a lifetime of fishing.

I just wish Danny Humic and the Presti brothers had been there to see it.

Chapter 4

Perfect: A Fly Tier's Beginnings

EARLY IN *A RIVER RUNS THROUGH IT*, Norman Maclean observes that when he was a boy growing up in Montana circa World War I, his family considered fly fishing a religion. When I was a kid in Western New York in the late 1950s, men fished with stiff casting rods from wooden boats in the wide and swift Niagara River, and boys who wanted to be men fished that way too. Our fathers loved their sport dearly, but they were not men inclined to metaphor, and no one could mistake the industrial Niagara for a cathedral in any case. As I understood it, fishing was more like a side job than a religion.

Over those childhood summers we drifted from the steel mills of Lackawanna, at the mouth of Lake Erie, all the way down past the big GM plant and the graphite and chemical factories that lined the river shore nearly to the rapids above the great Niagara Falls itself. We fished for smallmouths and walleyes, yellow perch and rock bass. But I longed for trout, those pretty little speckled creatures of the Great North Woods: the Adirondack Mountains, two hundred miles away, Maine or Labrador, even farther out of my reach. I studied pictures of those beautiful rivers and those beautiful fish and I started tying flies, anticipating the day I would be a trout fisherman—a fly fisherman.

When my best friend and next-door neighbor Danny Humic and I were in fourth or fifth grade, Danny got the first fly-tying kit I had ever seen. It came in a small cardboard carton gaily illustrated with images of classic East Coast trout and Atlantic salmon flies. Inside was a minimal assortment of feathers and fur and chenille and silk floss, a cheap stamped metal vise, flimsy tin hackle pliers, a chunk of bee's wax, and a few packets of hooks. In the tiny kitchen of the tiny GI Bill house that the Humics lived in next door to my almost identical tiny home, Danny and I clamped that vise to the chrome legged, Formica-topped table, tuned in WKBW (50 thousand watts of power!) broadcasting from downtown Buffalo, and tied our first flies, listening to the Shirelles inquiring if we'd still love them tomorrow.

Using straight eyed, #2, heavy-forged hooks with barbs like harpoons, we tied flies designed not for fly fishing per se, but for the drift rigs we fished with on the big Niagara River at the end of our street. We had no bobbin, so we snipped a foot-long piece of silk thread, rubbed a little bee's wax on it, wrapped it around the hook shank and clamped the hackle pliers onto the tag end so that the thread hung straight down below the vise. We tied in a broad blade of goose quill for the tail—usually orange or yellow—and heavy chenille in the same color for the body. We eschewed any sort of wing and simply wound a big, webby hen hackle (also of a matching color) at the neck and piled on a heap of half hitches and a gob of Mrs. Humic's nail polish to form a bulky, rock-hard head.

Around this time, Danny's father, who was an avid fisherman (unlike my own father), bought a modern aluminum car-top skiff and a 7.5 horsepower Mercury outboard. He promised to take Danny and me out on the Niagara River, where, he assured us, we would catch all sorts of fish using those simple, monochromatic flies he called Yellow Sallies or Orange Sallies. They obviously were not intended to represent insects, nor were they going to be presented to the fish in a way approximating natural insect behavior. Per Mr. Humic's instructions, we attached each fly onto the spring-locking eye at the tail end of a light wire, Indiana-style spinner. We were simply adding a little color to the hook on a spinning lure, but it felt like fly tying to me.

I was still in grade school, still using a bait-casting outfit, and not yet seduced by those sexy new French open-faced spinning reels just beginning to show up in the ads in the *Outdoor Life* and *Field and Stream* magazines—which I read devotedly. Danny's father would own the first Mitchell 300 reel I ever saw. I owned the old Ocean City level-wind casting reel loaded with black Dacron that I had caught my first fish on—a shiner. As I said, my father was not interested in fishing, but he recognized that I was crazy about the sport for reasons inexplicable by genetics and he bought me that outfit in a tackle shop in the Finger Lakes on a family vacation when I was four or five years old. I could cast about twelve feet with it, producing a mind-boggling crow's-nest of a backlash every single time, no matter how carefully I attempted to thumb the whirling spool.

No matter. Fishing out of Mr. Humic's boat, I had only to put on a heavy sinker and lower the line straight down over the gunwales and into the river. We may have been tying something approximating flies, but we were not fly fishing.

This was the drill: We tied the black Dacron line from our reels to one eyelet of a brass three-way swivel, then attached a two-foot monofilament leader to the second eye of the swivel. At the business end of the monofilament leader, we knotted on the Indiana spinner tarted up with one of our orange or yellow "Sally" flies. From the remaining, unoccupied, brass eye of the three-way swivel we dangled a quarter-ounce bell sinker on a short length of white cotton butcher's string. Drifting down the Niagara, that sinker bumped the bottom while the fly-enhanced spinner trailed along behind it, just above the rocks and weeds, spinning and flashing. If the sinker snagged, the cheap white cotton string broke before the heavy Dacron did, so the only thing we lost was the sinker. Since we molded the sinkers ourselves down in Danny's basement using scraps of old lead pipefittings that we melted on his father's Coleman stove, the sinkers were essentially free. Children working with molten lead! Today we are worried that a baby might bump up against trace amounts of it in century-old paint on a door casing. My second grade teacher showed us how to roll pure mercury around in the palms of our hands. I don't even want to think about what our fathers were handling in the factories. Ah, those halcyon 1950s.

We were not naïve about our chances of catching fish. To hedge our bets and make sure the spinner with the fly attached to it was as effective as possible before sending it over the rail of the skiff and into the river, we always added one more thing: a really big nightcrawler, hooked once through the collar so that it dangled enticingly from the rear end of the fly we had tied. Using this spinner-fly-worm concatenation, I caught everything from white bass to northern pike, and even one undersized but unforgettably ferocious musky during the first ten years of my fishing life. All the while I waited for the day I would actually get to wave a fly rod over a bubbling brook full of trout, just like the writers in the outdoor magazines.

My great uncle Joe—who was the first educated person in our family—sealed my destiny to become a fly fisher. Uncle Joe was a scientist and a professor who had worked in the distant Great American Desert as a biologist for the state of Arizona. He was my grandmother's brother, and an actual visionary, I now realize. I remember him futilely trying to explain to me something he called a binary system, by moving a couple of pennies around with his fingertips on the spaghetti-stained tablecloth after a family dinner at my grandmother's house. He claimed this binary stuff was going to be a big thing in the future. I was nine or ten years old and had watched the Disney version of the future with its jet packs and flying automobiles and I did not think binary numbers and these computer thingies he was always talking about were nearly as interesting. By the time my grandmother served dessert, poor intelligent Uncle Joe had given up and I was happy to be excused so I could go watch Lawrence Welk and the Lennon Sisters, or maybe Elvis on the Ed Sullivan show.

My great uncle did help make me a fly fisher, however, by giving my father a copy of *Trout*, Ray Bergman's seminal 1938 sport fishing tome. Uncle Joe was the first adult I knew to acknowledge the existence of traditional fly fishing. He was also, by the time he gave us that book, a patient in what we referred to as the "State Mental Hospital" in Buffalo. While there in the hospital, Uncle Joe had somehow become convinced that my father, his nephew, was interested in the sport. On the inside cover of the famous Bergman book—one of the few family heirlooms I possess—is an inscription encouraging my father to share his "love for the gentle art of fishing" with his children. It is written in pen in a hesitant hand with several crossed-out words, as though my uncle, who had endured electroshock therapy and god only knows what mind-scrambling drugs, had gotten confused a couple times in the middle of the missive. Beneath his shaky script you can still see the rubber-stamped words O.T. DEPT. / J.N. ADAMS HOSPT. At the bottom of the page, Uncle Joe wrote, "I hope the 'flies' don't get you!" I hopefully interpret that to mean he had hung on to a sense of humor in spite of his dreadful depression and its gruesome treatment.

The flies did not get to my father, who never came down with the fly-fishing affliction. But they stung me badly. The places Ray Bergman described may have been far beyond a young boy's reach, but those fly patterns weren't. Or so I believed. I lay in my bed each night during the long Niagara Frontier winters intently studying the beautiful Dr. Edgar Burke color fly plates. To discourage anyone from ripping one of the pages out to have it framed, each one was rubber stamped with the words O.T. DEPT./ J.N. ADAMS HOSPT.

I was enthralled. The names of the fly patterns resonated with a kind of tweedy, Teddy Roosevelt outdoorsiness that I longed to be part of. An old style wet fly with a golden pheasant tail and bright yellow wing was labeled the Gibson Girl; another, the Jennie Lind. There were patterns named simply Adirondack and Catskill and St. Lawrence, evoking the East Coast landscapes of the early years of the sport. A decade later I would discover the whole Dan Bailey/ Rocky Mountain, muddler-gulping brown trout milieu. But at this time all I wanted was to puff on a smoldering pipe and watch one small Maine brookie rise to a Light Cahill or a Fan Wing Coachman—a fly that I, of course, had tied myself.

There were flies named after great men of the sport: Seth Green and the author Ray Bergman, for example. There was the Royal Wulff, a moniker suiting our reigning king. The artist managed to sneak in a few of his own creations: on plate #12 there is a streamer tied with a silver tinsel body, a white hackle wing, and a peacock sword tail called the Dr. Burke.

Bergman's *Trout* is without a question one of the most influential books I've ever read; it is probably the one that instilled ideas and values (superficial as they may be) in me more than any other. Of course, if I'm ever very famous—for God knows what reason—and I'm asked that question about literary influences, I'm going to pull my chin thoughtfully and name *Moby Dick,* or *One Hundred Years of Solitude.*

I read *Trout* over and over, or at least I looked at those drawings repeatedly. And in doing so I started to realize how far I had to go to be a real fly fisherman, and a fly tier. I remember coming across the plate depicting the authentic Yellow Sally. The classic pattern, with its svelte silk body, fine hackle fiber tail, and delicate yellow wing, looked nothing like the bulging chenille-bodied brutes that I impaled nightcrawlers on and drowned in the Niagara. I became obsessed with tying real trout flies, imagining an updated edition of Bergman's book one day containing there among the famous fly patterns, the Chiappone Special, or Rich's Delight.

I sent away to Herter's for fine wire fly hooks and carried them over to Danny Humic's house and attempted to copy some of the traditional patterns in the Bergman book. But the recipes called for things like barred mallard tips and jungle cock eyes. Danny's kit contained mostly foot long goose quills and chunks of dyed bucktail, both of which were handy for brightening our spinners and calling attention to the worms we had dangling from them. However, they were of little use to the wannabe tier of a Housatonic Quill or a Pale Evening Dun. What I needed were golden pheasant tippets, speckled mandarin duck feathers, ostrich and peacock herls. What I also needed was a place to fish for trout. But for the moment my goal was to construct one real trout fly, so I concentrated on getting the materials.

Like many neophyte fly tiers, I experimented with Labrador retriever hair and orange cat fur, with limited success. Rabbit and muskrat were fairly easy to obtain locally, and grouse and pheasant feathers were common enough, as many of the men on our street hunted avidly. Of course, there were always plenty of large Norway rats down at the cement docks at the Niagara River at the end of my street, free for the taking by a boy with a pellet gun. But rat fur was short and greasy and never lost its rodenty creepiness. Once, I found a dead squirrel in my driveway lying there like a gift from heaven, a neat round hole burned into one hind leg where it had touched the power line overhead. I may still have some of that tail somewhere in my fly-tying desk.

It was not just the rare birds that were a problem. Certainly peafowl and ostrich were a little scarce in Niagara County, but even a decent rooster hackle was impossible to find. In the industrial neighborhood where I lived, chickens were no more common than jungle cocks. I despaired of ever having the materials I needed.

Then one winter night, lying in bed, not yet asleep, I felt a small sharp pain in my cheek and discovered the quill end of a tiny feather poking out from the fabric of the pillowcase. I tugged on it and found myself holding a lovely chicken hackle, creamy white with a dark brown band along the stem.

I crawled out of bed and neatly folded the hackle into a Kleenex, and set the tissue on the little nightstand between my bed and my brother Michael's. I put a small rubber dinosaur, an ankylosaurus, on top of it to keep the feather from drifting off when the furnace kicked on. In the morning before leaving for school I opened the tissue and bent the hackle stem around my finger once again just to see those hairy fibers stand up like the buggy little insect legs they would imitate. Then I carefully rewrapped it, set it back on the nightstand and spent the day sketching dry flies in the margins of my notebook while Mrs. Neuman attempted to interest us in fractions and adverbs and ancient wars fought long ago by people who probably didn't even fish.

Despite the fact that I had been sleeping on a pillow filled with chicken feathers for years, finding that hackle right there on my pillowcase seemed as miraculous as if I had discovered the face of Jesus there. After school, I ran home through falling snow and raced into my bedroom and straight to the nightstand where I found the little ankylosaurus sitting alone, his rubber feet planted firmly on the varnished pine surface. There was no sign of the Kleenex with the precious feather inside. My mother had tidied up.

"I thought it was a used tissue," she said, peeling an eggplant at the kitchen counter of our tiny two-bedroom house.

I groaned. I sulked. I moped.

The Kleenex was out in the driveway at the bottom of one of our three garbage cans, under who knew how many pounds of household detritus. The precious feather was entombed now beneath piles of crumpled newspapers and discarded homework, Campbell's Soup cans and empty cereal boxes, fragments of pork chop bones and strands of pasta sticky with congealing meat sauce.

I acted as though it had been the last feather on the last chicken on earth. "It was perfect!" I groaned.

My father came in from work in the middle of the drama. "A feather?" he said, stomping snow off his boots in the doorway, hanging up his coat, his hat. "Like from a bird?"

I tried to explain. But to a man who worked in a graphite plant all week and then played accordion at weddings on the weekends to put food on the table and shoes on the feet of his seven children, the appeal of fly fishing, let alone fly tying, remained a mystery all his life. I was in the middle of a whiny tirade about the scarcity of hackle feathers in my life when my mother sighed, "Oh for Pete's sake, Richard." She squeezed past my father and out the kitchen door, as though she could not stand the pressure of my emoting inside the tight confines of that little kitchen any longer.

My father said, "Are you happy now? You made your mother go out into a snowstorm. For a feather. In her apron!"

I said, "I'll go get her."

But I hadn't gone two steps before she came back in through that door, new snow clumped in her hair. She was holding a wadded Kleenex between her thumb and fingertip. She laid it on the kitchen table. My father and I leaned around her, watching as she gently peeled back the crumpled corners. There was the magnificent hackle feather, still nestled in the tissue, kinked, but otherwise intact.

"Now," my mother said, "do you mind if I make dinner before the baby wakes up?" There was always a baby in the house. She rolled her eyes and turned to wash her hands in the kitchen sink.

My father picked up the hackle feather and held it up to the ceiling light, studying it. The stem was bent into a ninety degree dogleg. He said, "You call this perfect?"

I went up behind my mother at the sink, wrapped my arms around her waist, gave her a hug, and thanked her.

"Yes," I said, to my father. "It's perfect."

If the Shirelles weren't playing, they should have been.

Chapter 5

The King and I

IN 1653, IZAAC WALTON, ONE of the earliest commentators on the world of fishing, called salmon the "king of fish" in his famous tour de force, *The Compleat Angler*. Almost exactly three hundred years later, I sat on the living room floor of my best friend Danny Humic's house in the industrial Rust Belt city of Niagara Falls, NY, watching what had to be one of the earliest TV fishing shows. On the screen, Lee Wulff, angling guru and raconteur, stood grinning at the camera somewhere in remote Quebec or Labrador, holding up an Atlantic salmon as long as my nine-year-old leg. The fish looked like a chrome-plated torpedo with eyes.

Yes, the fish was fabulous, but I certainly didn't think of it as kingly. At that age the allure of royalty was beyond me: I was more interested in King Kong than King Arthur. What impressed me most was the absence of houses, telephone poles, and, most importantly, factories along that heavenly wild Canadian river. I lived one block inland from the Niagara River, and a few blocks upstream from the big plants lining its shore: Hooker Chemical, DuPont, Union Carbide, International Graphite. Day and night, they spewed black soot and sulfurous fumes into the air, and God knows what into the river. The nearest Atlantic salmon streams were hundreds of miles to the east, the nearest Pacific salmon, thousands of miles west.

ALTHOUGH MY FATHER HAD LITTLE interest in the sport, I became a fisherman for some reason. One block to the north of our street, the boys my age played Wiffle ball, joined Little League, became high school jocks; one block to the south, the boys leaned into the engines of their fathers' cars and counted the days to their learner's permits. On our street, boys fished. All of which would have been positively idyllic, except that we fished on the pollution-ravaged Niagara.

One morning, on our walk to school, a friend and fishing buddy named Bob Hawkins announced that his family was moving to Vancouver, British Columbia. He produced what must have been a field guide to western fishes, and we studied the drawings of the five Pacific salmon species he'd soon be hauling in. The beautiful green-headed, red-bodied, spawning sockeye fascinated me. Oh, Bob Hawkins would definitely catch some of those—the lucky bastard. British Columbia, on the distant opposite edge of the continent, was clearly a province in the Kingdom of the Salmon. It never occurred to me that Vancouver was a real city, much larger than my own town, and that there would be all kinds of buildings there too—perhaps even factories. Salmon lived there, or near there. That was all I needed to know. Longing for the day I would catch, or even simply see, a live salmon, I focused on the next best thing, and the only alternative within reach: the King of Fish's vassal, the Trout.

When we were in fifth grade, Danny Humic's father took Danny and me to a children's fishing derby at a man-made pond somewhere south of Buffalo. There might have been a hundred of us kids encircling that little pond in the dawn mist when the sheriff fired the starting shot. A hundred spinning lures and baited hooks sailed out—many crisscrossing, of course. My first trout, a hatchery-raised brown, maybe ten inches long, came in fifteenth place.

For days afterward, I kept it in the refrigerator and proudly showed it to anyone I could corner. I wouldn't let my mother cook it. At the end of the week, sick of the odor, she apologetically tossed it in the trash.

For the next ten years, trout would be the closest things to salmon I would see. Yes, they are lovely little fish, among the most beautiful in the world, as Izaac Walton and every other fishing writer since has declared many times over, but they lack the grandeur, the sovereign status of their liege lords. And the hatchery-stocked waters that trout inhabited—at least those within range of my weekend fishing trips with Danny and his father—were not the grandly wild salmon rivers of my dreams. Not even close.

Now, if I'd been more adventurous, I might have traveled straight to salmon country after graduating from high school and college. Another friend, Jerry Presti, did just that. Some time before the Marine Mammal Protection Act of 1972, Jerry loaded his fishing rods and hunting rifles into a VW Bus and drove four thousand miles from Niagara Falls to Alaska. He shot a moose and—for some reason I can't even fathom today—a harbor seal the size of Danny Humic's TV console. He had the dead pinniped stuffed and displayed it in the very small living room of the Presti house on 68th Street.

Nearly forty-five years later, what I remember most about Jerry's Alaskan adventure was the 8mm home movie of him catching wild silver salmon in a misty rain forest river, far from the factories of our town. Yes, I wanted so badly to do that too, but instead I dropped out of school and married very young, and the Kingdom of the Salmon remained unreachable for a long, long while. With no education and a wife and daughters to support, I painted houses and commercial buildings, and even the chemical tanks of the big factories I'd grown up alongside. I spent my twenties climbing steel towers and pipe racks overlooking the Niagara, trying, in a way, to see the wild rivers over the horizon.

And then the mountain came to Mohammed. Sort of.

* * *

By the late 1960s, native game fish in the Great Lakes (musky, bass, walleye, and lake trout) were nearly extirpated by overfishing, pollution, habitat destruction, and predation by non-indigenous sea lampreys. With the large, top-of-the-food-chain fish depleted, the population of another invasive species, herring-like alewives, exploded so rapidly the lakes couldn't support them; they died off each year by the millions, their rotting carcasses fouling beaches. In 1966, the State of Michigan began stocking Pacific coho (silver) salmon in Lake Michigan to prey on the alewives. The program proved so successful, and the big game fish so popular with sportsmen, New York State followed suit, planting coho and Chinook (king) salmon in Lake Ontario and Lake Erie tributary streams.

Suddenly I had salmon in my own backyard. Problem solved. Dreams attained.

Well, not exactly.

To begin with, the newly introduced salmon could not reproduce in most local creeks, where warm summer water temperatures and shallow gradients prevented the oxygenation needed for viable eggs. That meant it was a put-and-take, hatchery-dependent fishery. And the sluggish streams—formerly habitat mostly for sunfish and suckers—didn't exactly meet my Kingdom of the Salmon expectations either, no matter how many lordly fish the State dumped in. An additional pall was cast over the whole enterprise by the official warnings that salmon from Lake Erie and Lake Ontario streams could contain PCBs, dioxin, mirex, and other potential carcinogens. My hometown, Niagara Falls, is also the home of Love Canal, one of the country's first Superfund toxic waste cleanup sites. All in all, it was a rather incongruous and dystopian realm for the King of Fish. Picture the British Royals relocating to a coal town in Wales.

Still—salmon, right under my nose. The pragmatic thing to do was fish for them.

Sometime in the early 1970s, I caught my first salmon, a fifteen-pound Chinook, in the Niagara River Gorge, just downstream from the huge Niagara Mohawk Power Corporation turbine house and directly across the river from the infamously filthy American Cyanamid plant on the Canadian shore. It was late in the fall, and the hook-jawed male fish was intent on finding a mate before dying, blissfully unaware of the futility of that whole enterprise. But, unlike salmon pictured in books, this one had not turned an exotic red and green; its whole body was a sickly black. I was unsure how tasty a deteriorating salmon from the less-than-pristine Niagara might be. But, unwilling to just throw it away after dreaming about this moment since I was a child, I brined and smoked that fish—probably adding more carcinogens to those already in it. My mother, always a good sport, served it for an appetizer with Thanksgiving dinner that year. Nobody died. At least not right away.

Over the next decade, I caught salmon from Lake Ontario, Lake Erie, and Lake Huron streams. In a way, I was thankful that they were all darkening spawners; it was easier to simply declare a fish too far gone to eat than try to figure out how toxic it might be. As much as I longed to adore them, the non-native salmon—planted in the Great Lakes to solve a trash fish problem—would always seem misplaced royalty, and unhealthy to boot. And that was my worshipful/fearful relationship with the King of Fish for all of the 1970s.

* * *

By 1979, the transplanted Pacific salmon were thriving in the Great Lakes, but my first marriage was foundering. So was the economy of western New York. Divorced and in need of steady employment, I transferred my membership in the International Brotherhood of

Painters and Allied Trades to the local union in Las Vegas, Nevada, America's perennial boomtown. There, I found plenty of work as a paperhanger in the endless casino expansions of that time. But a move to the Great American Desert did not get me any closer to wild salmon. Three years in the bleak alkali wastelands of southern Nevada left me aching more than ever for the great northern woods and rivers of my childhood dreams. In 1982 I moved my union book to Anchorage, Alaska, another boomtown—but, this time, one built smack in the middle of the Kingdom of the Salmon.

I caught my first wild, native Alaskan salmon that spring, a king about the size of the one I had caught ten years earlier in the Niagara gorge. This one, taken from the beautiful little Ninilchik River, a mile upstream from the saltwater of Cook Inlet, was every bit as silvery bright as Lee Wulff's Atlantic salmon had looked on Danny's TV, thirty years prior. It came out of the lovely little stream, twisting and thrashing in the spring sun like the magnificent game fish it was. And this fish had probably never seen a PCB or dioxin molecule in its life.

I have been fishing for kings and every other species of Pacific salmon ever since. I've caught chum salmon on the remote Yukon–Kuskokwim Delta, huge silver salmon on Kodiak Island, and diminutive humpies in the Aleutians. Over the years, I've caught hundreds of sockeye on the world-famous Kenai River—not the strange green-headed creatures of Bob Hawkins's field guide, but chrome bright fish fresh from the sea, one of the greatest food fish in the world.

In the mid-1980s, driven by my desire to fish, and my second wife's love of the boreal forests of the Kenai Peninsula, we bought three acres of dense white spruce forest along the Anchor River, 200 miles south of Anchorage. There, we quite literally built a life around salmon fishing, starting with a tent platform in the late '80s, where my wife canned our fresh-caught sockeyes on a Coleman stove, and finishing with a two-story home with a cook's kitchen and a spare bedroom for fly-fishing guests. In 2002, when my wife got a job at the high school in the nearby town of Homer, we moved to the Anchor River.

Though the house is about the same distance from the Anchor as the one I grew up in was from the Niagara, the nearest thing to a factory might be one of the salmon canneries in the town of Kenai, about fifty miles to the north. It's an idyllic setting, a little piece of the Kingdom of the Salmon as I always envisioned it. But after thirty-two years of fishing for salmon, I've noticed lately that I spend more time than I used to thinking about the last chapter of their life cycles, the high-speed senescence that overtakes them when they enter fresh water. Maybe it was receiving my first Social Security check in the mail this September, just when the Anchor River gravel bars and river banks lay littered with decomposing salmon carcasses, and the last of the late spawners writhed and gasped in the shallows around my hip boots, their flesh sliding off them, their heads covered in white fungus.

Not to get too morbid, but in a sure sign that the next kingdom I'll be entering is my own dotage, I even wrote a poem about it. Well, a limerick, actually.

Spawners

The salmon, most noble of trout,
mates rotting from tail to snout.
With fungus-blind eyes,
it has sex once and dies.
I think I'd as soon go without.

My impertinence notwithstanding, I love the King of Fish and the places where they live. I love to catch them, and I love to cook and eat them. Let's face it: for a working-class kid from Love Canal, they are as close to royalty as I'm ever going to get.

PART II
Into the Woods

CHAPTER 6

Oblivious

"I'm gonna knock his head clean off!"
—Br'er Bear, *Song of the South*

ONE OF THE EARLIEST MEMORIES I have is of my mother reading to me from a Little Golden Book designed to teach preschoolers the alphabet by way of the Noah's Ark story. On page one, Noah gathered two apes—or aardvarks maybe, something starting with the letter A. I don't remember. On the last page two zebras climbed up the gangplank to the big boat under Noah's benevolent, animal-loving gaze just as the rain clouds opened up for the first of forty extremely wet days and nights. What I remember most is the letter B, spoken for by two enormous brown bears, which, according to this version, Noah acquired in a place called the Great North Woods. The Great North Woods! I was a goner. Along with Never Never Land and that island where the little boys in Pinocchio went to gamble and smoke cigars, the Great North Woods became a fantasy destination I had to see, had to live in.

The artwork for that page in the little book remains in my heart and mind today: Behind those two lucky bruins who got the species-saving boat ride from Noah, a forest of pointy topped conifers was rendered iconically as tall, green, Christmas tree triangles. I hadn't even been bitten by the fishing bug yet (that would come one or two years later), but I wanted to go to the Great North Woods. I wanted to see brown bears. It would have to wait. I was four years old with no way to get there. Besides, my mother didn't allow me to get close to dangerous wild animals.

At that time, we hadn't yet moved to the house near the river, and we still lived in an old neighborhood in downtown Niagara Falls. While Western New York State indeed sits at a relatively northerly latitude, there was nothing "great" about what few wooded vacant lots remained in the old industrial city, and there were no bears at all in Niagara County by the 1950s. What there was however was the Great Bear Market on Pine Avenue in the middle of the ethnic Italian neighborhood. The Great Bear was a family-owned place, but it was large and rather ambitious, a precursor to the big chain supermarkets that would replace it a few decades later. It stood out as something quite modern among the more traditional mom-and-pop stores catering to the immigrant population there. Take the Stinky Store, for example. This is the name my little sister Claudia and I had for Latina Italian Imports. Each time our mother took us in there our tiny, sensitive noses were assaulted by the stench of hard cheeses and sopressata salamis and God only knows what other odiferous Old World products they had hanging from the ceiling of the crammed little store. We preferred the clean, modern Great Bear Market filled with familiar Campbell soups and Wonder Bread and Maxwell House coffee that our generation embraced and preferred over the pig's feet and Sicilian snails that Latina Italian Imports offered. Mostly, I loved the sign over the Great Bear Market's door featuring a giant bear standing on its hind legs. It might have been a polar bear, now that I think of it, but who cares? I wanted to see real bears. Wild bears. Big ones. I wanted to get close to them, just like Noah—who I considered a lucky bastard for having a whole boatful of wild animals of his own. It would be almost thirty years before I moved to Alaska to fish its great northern rivers and had my wish come true many times over.

If you are going to fish coastal Alaskan rivers, you are going to fish with bears. Whether you see them or not, they're somewhere nearby. And how you feel about that is going to fall somewhere on a scale between paranoid white-knuckle terror that makes your every hour on a salmon-filled stream an endless nail-biting nightmare and, at the other extreme, a foolish obliviousness that puts you and everyone around you in danger of death by tooth and claw. I hate to admit it, but I'm pretty much the best example of the fool at the latter end of the scale you'll ever find. One of the reasons I fish is because it is very cheap therapy. When I'm up to my wader belt in a trout stream, casting, I tend to forget about everything and anything even potentially unpleasant in my life or around me. Unfortunately, that includes bears. Which is why I've ended up close to bears more times than my four-year-old self ever dreamed I would.

There is no such thing as being simply "close" to coastal Alaskan brown bears. There is only "far far away" from them or "way too fucking close." In June of 1989, on a trip to the Brooks River in Katmai National Park, I got way too close to a brown bear for the first time. I had just tangled with a Katmai rainbow trout far too heavy and rambunctious for the light line I had brought with me. I was sitting by myself on a grassy bankside tussock, tying on a new tippet, my neoprene-clad legs dangling in the water at the foot of a tall cutbank. A few hundred yards upstream, the famous Brooks Falls—often pictured on calendars lined with enormous bears snapping at leaping sockeye salmon—rushed and rumbled in the sunny afternoon air, lulling me into the kind of stupefied serenity that river music and sunshine can produce. Distracted by the possibility of hooking another big rainbow, I was *lost in thought*, as the cliché goes—but, more accurately, lack of thought is probably closer—when, over the rushing water, I heard a snort above and behind me. I turned and looked up the steep cutbank. An enormous bear, whom I would later learn was the dominant bear on the river and had been named Diver by the rangers, stood at the brink of the cutbank, about ten feet above me, looking down. At me.

Diver, now long deceased, was estimated to weigh eight hundred pounds when he emerged from hibernation each spring, and well over a thousand by autumn after consuming sixty or seventy pounds of salmon each day all summer. Sitting on the ground as I was, looking up at him from that low angle, he looked like a dirigible in a fur coat. He pulled his lips back and showed me his teeth, in what I hoped was a smile. I could almost hear him doing the math: one 180-pound fly fisherman equals thirty sockeye salmon averaging six pounds apiece. Plus, he wouldn't even have to dive for the meat. Hmmm.

Being the "dominant" bear on the river meant that he was the biggest, toughest, scariest animal within a community of thirty or forty very big, tough, and scary animals. It also meant that he could walk, swim, or fish anywhere he wanted to, whenever he wanted to—unless, of course, somebody cared to challenge him.

I stood, my intestines twisting, recalling the park rangers' rule: Do not run when confronted by a bear. Run? I was wearing chest waders, standing in fast water at the base of a dirt cliff. There was nowhere to run. My natural inclination was to plunge downstream and let the river carry me away from the monster, but there was nothing but deep water in that direction, and I can't swim wearing a bathing suit, let alone in waders. So, I stepped aside and slogged a few yards upstream against the current, yanking out handfuls of grasses from the base of the cutbank with one hand, gripping my fly rod in the other. Diver waited for me to move out of his way, slid down the bank in an avalanche of pebbles, walked right over the tussock I had been sitting on a moment before, and dropped into the river. I could have touched him with the tip of my rod. Another rule: Stay fifty yards away from any bear, a hundred yards from a sow with cubs. My fly rod is exactly three yards long. I could see I was going to have to be a little more vigilant. I could also see that vigilance was not my strongest trait. It's still not.

Last month, I went camping in Katmai again for the twentieth time (I missed one year in the '90s for some reason I now forget). It should be no surprise that I have not become a whole lot more careful in those intervening two decades. In fact, twenty years of camping alongside the Brooks River bears has only made me even more foolishly comfortable with them, and I'll admit right now that my luck is going to run out one of these days. Unlike the late, now famous, Timothy Treadwell, I do not think that the bears are my buddies or my pets, but I do love seeing them again and again—especially up way too close. They are a big reason I came to Alaska in the first place—one of the things that make living and fishing in the Great Land great.

So, this summer I got to see some big bears again up way too close. My wife and I flew out to Katmai for our twentieth Brooks River anniversary. There we met up with old friends already settled into the campground. When we first camped in the lovely cottonwood grove there on the shore of Naknek Lake twenty-one years ago, the bears roamed among us at will. They appeared suddenly, showing up at the picnic tables, disrupting our dinners; they stomped past our tents in the middle of the night, sniffing and huffing and sending jolts of adrenaline shooting through us as we huddled in our sleeping bags. It was good scary fun.

One night in the early years, I fished until the near-dark twilight of the Alaskan summer threw long shadows across the forest path around midnight. All the others in our party had given up and gone to bed hours before, but I was still young and in my "more is better" mode. Exhausted from a very long day of wading and fishing, I stumbled back to camp, alone, head down, wading shoes dragging. Apparently, some bears are no more cautious than I am. I was within sight of our tent—in which my wife was lying in her sleeping bag, reading, and possibly wondering where I was so late, and how much of my remains my life insurance policy required as proof of death—when I ran right into a big bear, also bumbling along, head down. It could have been Diver. It was too dark to tell, and not the right moment for introductions. We both yelped, and jumped back. I froze. The bear ran the other way, missed our tent by a couple feet, and stopped. It stood on its hind legs, looming over the tent trying to see what the heck it had collided with. I called out to my wife, "Honey, don't come out of the tent right now." Later she said that when the bear dropped down onto its front paws, maybe six feet away from her on the other side of the thin nylon wall, she felt the ground shake under its weight.

As I said: good, scary fun.

Today an electric fence surrounds the tent camping area, offering a feeling of security—no matter how close the bears come to the camp. We sleep much more soundly, but some of the thrill is gone too. Inside the fence we are the caged animals; the bears wander past freely, like zoo-goers. Maybe it's better this way.

This year, on our first evening in camp, a young sow with a single cub visited. The rangers said the big cub is two and a half years old; he is nearly as big as his mother and obviously needs to be sent out into the world, but the mom is apparently not ready to let go of her first child. (I was a first child myself—I know how charming we can be.) The sow and the huge cub stopped to roll around on the sandy beach in front of the campground. We stood inside the fence and oohed and ahhed and took pictures of them. They soon ambled off toward the river, probably checking to see if the salmon had started running yet.

The first night celebrations ran a little long and the whiskey a little low, and the next morning I awoke very late to find that my friends had already had breakfast and set off to the river to fish for trout. All the fly rods in camp and every pair of waders but mine were gone from the gear shelter. I was moving slowly, aching from the night on the ground in spite of the high-tech Therm-a-Rest pads beneath my none-too-fit body. I took my morning painkillers. (Almost everyone in camp is on the unfortunate side of sixty now; there are enough meds in our tents to start a M*A*S*H unit.) I was putting on my waders when the same sow and cub walked past along the beach, once more heading toward the Brooks River, a quarter mile away. I watched them again, with that same mix of awe and dread and gratitude for the chance to see them, another feeling I get whenever the big bears are near. By the time I left the campground and walked to the river I had forgotten they were in the area. The sun was shining and I was going fishing. My friends were already out there somewhere catching trout like mad, I believed. Who cares if some giant omnivores are roaming around in the brush? I'm talking about fat, wild Alaskan rainbows. I hurried the quarter mile from the campground to the river.

Standing on the footbridge at the mouth of the Brooks River where it flows into Naknek Lake, I could see my friend Bill and his wife Deb fishing a little ways upstream. Instead of following the gravel bars along the winding river, I decided to take a shortcut through the tall grass in a direct path to them. On the other side of the river, at the far end of the bridge, there is a bear-viewing platform about ten feet high for visitors who want to look at the bears but have no desire to climb into the river and fish alongside them for some reason. In other words, the sane visitors. The platform was full of such bear-viewers and photographers. There were a couple rangers.

I left the path and strode out into the tall grass on a beeline for the oxbow where my friends were fishing, but I only got about halfway to the river when Deb saw me approaching and began shouting: "Rich! Bear! Rich! Bear!" I have to say that hearing your name urgently placed in the same sentence fragment as the word "bear" is not comforting. Not when you are knee-deep in boot-sucking mud and can't see over the grass in front of you. I hit the brakes. The sow and the big cub—which all the people on the platform had been watching me approach, but not warning me about—stood up on their hind legs a few yards in front of me. Without the electric fence between us, they looked a lot bigger and far less cuddly. The platform erupted with laughter as I backtracked and took a roundabout route to the oxbow. Forget the hundred yards from a sow and her cubs rule; I had foolishly come within a couple dozen feet of them. Now, I don't mind being the class clown, or the comic relief character, and I do realize that the rangers can't prevent every careless idiot such as myself from getting chewed to shreds because of our own stupidity, but a little shout-out from the platform about the bears I was heading for might have been in order in this case.

That particular sow with the oversized cub was a single mom raising the bruin equivalent of a teenage boy, and she looked it. She was haggard and sort of weary-looking and seemed like she might be ready for an argument with anyone dumb enough to start one. Put yourself in her paws. She was getting no support from the father (doesn't even know who the father was), and worse, in fact knew that the father—or any other large male bear for that matter—would far more likely eat her teenage son than offer to help rearing him. She looked like she would certainly bite your head off if you rubbed her the wrong way. And in this case, those are not metaphors. A brown bear will often grab its victim by the head during an attack. And there is no right way to rub one.

A little fear of bears and other large carnivores is obviously a good idea when fishing in bear country. But you can't let it keep you home. In 1972 I went to the nearest thing to the Great North Woods I could reach at that time in my life. I was still living in Niagara Falls, married with one child, working in a paint store, painting houses on weekends for extra money. I was not going to Alaska any time soon. My young brother Marty and I did go camping in Algonquin Provincial Park on the Laurentian Plateau of Central Ontario, Canada, that spring. It was a place where a black bear had killed a couple young boys the year before. We were intrigued and more than a little frightened. But it was our first remote backcountry fishing trip and nothing as minor as a man-eating bear could stop us.

We canoed and portaged our way across a lake system until we were far from the one road that cuts across the southernmost corner of the big park. We fished, and we cooked trout on a wood fire, and slept in a cheap plastic tent in Army Surplus sleeping bags—no Therm-a-Rests—on the hard Precambrian bedrock. The condensation from our breath dripped on us all night long. It was May, and it got very dark in the middle of the night, and when we heard the chewing sounds start, just outside the tent, we knew that the killer black bear was working through our food supply on his way to us. We had no flashlight.

Marty was sixteen years old. Being his older brother, a married man and a father, I felt responsible for him. More senseless than brave, I led the way from the tent into the absolutely opaque blackness, lighting wooden matches and cupping them one after another in front of me trying to throw a little light on the fearsome beast that had come for us. We nearly tripped over the porcupine before we saw him, hunched under the overturned canoe, nibbling on one paddle. We did not have a gun. I have no idea what we thought we were going to do, or perhaps say, to the animal if it had, in fact, been a bear.

In my twenty trips to the Brooks River, and in all my foolishly close encounters with those bears there, I have never had a gun on my person. That is partly because I have no training and very little experience with guns (I hunted small game when I was a younger man), but it is also because guns have been prohibited in National Parks. Only recently, as I got older and less able to convince myself that I could climb a spruce tree if I needed to, have I begun carrying bear-repellent pepper spray. But this past winter the National Park regulations were amended to allow guns in the parks—to the extent that state laws allow them wherever the park is situated. That means guns are now permitted in all Alaska national parks. You are not allowed to discharge them. But there will be extenuating circumstances, you can be sure.

For example, in May, a camper shot and killed a bear in self-defense in Denali National Park. Maybe it is a coincidence that in the first month of the first summer that guns have been allowed, a bear needed to be shot in a park that gets tens of thousands of visitors each year and to the best of my knowledge has never had a fatal bear attack. What I do know is that someone is going to shoot a Brooks River bear, probably very soon. The inevitable way-too-close encounters are not for everyone. Twenty years ago, if I had been the kind of guy who was good with a gun, I would have shot Diver coming down that cutbank toward me looking for all the world like the giant predator he was. There has never been a bear attack of any kind in Brooks Camp in spite of the thousands of visitors there too. But I have a feeling there will be one as soon as there are enough people packing guns there.

About mid-week in my recent trip to Brooks Camp, my innate obliviousness once again put me in harm's way. Five of us set out to fish for pike in an old beaver pond maybe a hundred yards inland from the beach on Naknek Lake, about a mile from the camp. Half-way there we spotted a huge male bear walking toward us along the big lake's edge. We cut inland and bushwhacked through the alders and willows to the beaver pond, the big bear forgotten as soon as we started catching pike. I had drifted away from the others and was by myself, standing in hip-deep water by the huge beaver dam that had created the lake in the first place. There I cast a fly out into the deeper water where I hoped the biggest pike lurked. Casting a fly is one of the few truly pleasurable things a man my age can do repeatedly, for hours on end, without either hurting or embarrassing himself. Needless to say, I was not paying attention to anything around me.

Once again it was Deb who called out, "Rich! Bear!"

Maybe thirty feet away, a short cast with a fly rod, the enormous bear sidled across the top of the beaver dam. This was no juvenile delinquent cub or world-weary single mom sow. This was a trophy-sized male bear. There is a reason taxidermists mount bears on small mounds to make them look taller and scarier. It works. Looking upward at the animal there on top of the beaver house, perhaps six feet above my eye level, it looked like a Pleistocene monster: *Arctodus simus*, the nearly two-thousand-pound mega-carnivore of prehistory. It was a jaw-dropping moment, and I just stood there watching it walk past, until Deb barked, "Rich! Come on." I snapped out of my reverie and waded away from the big bear and back toward the company of my fellow meat snacks. There is safety in numbers, primarily because the odds improve that someone is paying attention. It is never I.

My wife has admitted that in the first few years of our relationship she credulously believed that when I drove right past the Safeway Store where we shopped several times a week, when I left the water running in the sink until it overflowed, when I went out to pick up a pizza and some beer and came home without the pizza, I might have been lost in profound thoughts. Somewhere along the line in our more than thirty years of marriage, it dawned on her that I may not be thinking at all. My mother used the old-fashioned saying that I "had my head in the clouds." My wife would locate my head somewhere much closer the ground and decidedly less ethereal.

Either way, I'll keep going back to Brooks Camp, unarmed and oblivious as ever, to wander among the fabulous bears, happily fishing, and stumbling over their huge furry hulks until one of them knocks my head clean off.

Postscript, August 5, 2015:
Coincidentally, while taking a break from revising this particular essay (written five or six years ago) for inclusion in this book, my

wife and I were in Upper Skilak Lake campground here on the Kenai Peninsula two days ago when a young woman had to be medivaced out by helicopter after being mauled by a brown bear.

The attack had occurred miles away from us, on the other side of the big lake. The young woman had been jogging with a friend on a trail near a lodge over there when they ran into the bear. The bear grabbed one woman, and the other one ran for help. Rescuers found the victim, bitten and scratched, but upright and walking down the trail after the bear left her on the ground. They brought her across the lake by boat to the campground where we were staying, because there was just enough room to land the chopper on the road into the camp. But we did not know any of that when the helicopter landed, and the medics began tending to an athletic young woman covered in blood.

For privacy reasons, I suppose, the medics wouldn't give us any information, so all we heard was that there'd been a mauling, and we assumed that since the victim was right there in camp, the bear was too. After she was flown off, gossip and hearsay and ill-informed chatter over the course of the evening only heightened the ominous sense of approaching tooth and claws. Who knew how close that bear was? Or why it had attacked? We've camped among bears for decades, and this was the first time we'd seen a victim of a mauling.

There are no electric fences around the campsites at Skilak Lake, and as my wife and I got into our sleeping bags in the fading summer light, I think it's fair to say we both wished we were safely ensconced in one of the several gigantic motor coaches in nearby sites instead of in our Big Agnes tent.

Still, it was a warm clear night, and we left the rain cover off the top of the tent in order to see the summer stars materialized in the darkening sky. And, of course, to keep one eye out for anything big coming our way.

In this morning's *Alaska Dispatch News*, the young woman was reported to be in "good" condition but still in the hospital. The bear, it said, had attacked in self-defense; the women had simply run up on top of it before it could get out of their way (which is what almost all bears do when approached by humans), and the animal lashed out in response.

It made me think of all the times I've blundered into them, and, simply put, have been undeservedly fortunate. Will I be a little more careful next summer out in Katmai, more vigilant, more responsible?

The big money is not on me.

Chapter 7

Egg-Sucking Everything

I suppose it is one of the more obvious lessons in life that the farther you travel from the birthplace of something truly noble and fine, the more license people will take with that fine thing, and the less recognizable it is bound to become. Certainly the most egregious example of this is the "Hawaiian-style" pizza, topped with canned pineapple and, for some reason I've never understood, Canadian bacon. But close behind that would have to be what we Alaskans have done to fly fishing.

After thirty-some years among my fellow philistines here in the Great Land, I might be too comfortable to recognize how low we've sunk, if not for a visit one recent summer to the Catskill Fly Fishing Center and Museum in Livingston Manor, New York, near the confluence of the fabled Beaver Kill and Willowemoc Creeks. Passing through on vacation, my wife and I stopped to peruse the glass cases cradling aging silk leaders, oxidizing single-action reels, flies so delicate and lifelike they seemed ready to lift off from the display velvet and seek a mate above the bucolic local streams there in the Fertile Crescent of our sport.

The place was as serious as the Vatican. Here lay the bones of saints, splinters from the True Cross. A group of pilgrims clad in pressed chinos and tasseled loafers whispered in awed reverence. I stepped behind a classic fly pattern display case to conceal my road Reeboks, my travel jeans; for the first time in my life I wished I had taken up pipe smoking. Before me in the case was a tiny Quill Gordon, tied by the eponymous Theodore Gordon himself, the father of American dry fly fishing. From its proud dun tail to its elegant wood duck wings it was a thing of unity, balance, and symmetry, and perhaps the quintessential Eastern trout fly. Truly something to be revered. But like a kid in church daydreaming of girlie mags, my mind drifted to our own Alaskan signature pattern, the Egg-Sucking Leech.

Does it imitate anything as delicate and ephemeral as a mayfly? Well, no. Essentially a huge purple Wooly Bugger with a ball of hot pink or red chenille tied in at the eye of the hook, it ostensibly mimics a bright purple leech attempting to swallow a feverishly swollen salmon egg. (In deference to those with delicate sensibilities I will not name the variation, on which the inflamed pink portion is located at the bend of the hook, i.e., the terminus of the "leech's" alimentary canal.) The fact that there are no purple leeches in Alaska, and that our ordinary green and black leeches do not, as far as I can tell, actually eat salmon eggs, raises the question of whether any self-respecting angler would want to be seen casting such a freakish creation under any circumstances. Yet this fly, or one of its variations (the Egg-Sucking Muddler, the Egg-Sucking Zonker, the Egg-Sucking Bead Head Krystal Flash, etc.), is invariably mentioned on nearly every Alaskan's list of must-have patterns, and for two good reasons: it catches fish like crazy, and it embodies our disdain for all things elegant, delicate, and traditional.

Alaskan fly boxes house some of the biggest, goofiest looking monstrosities outside of the World Wrestling Federation. The list includes such classics as the Alaskabou—a fistful of marabou lashed to an enormous, otherwise bare hook; the Bunny Bug—a fistful of rabbit fur lashed to an enormous, otherwise bare hook;

and, perhaps the mostly widely used of all, the Coho Fly—a two-toned fistful of colorful bucktail lashed to an enormous . . . well, you get the picture. Even when we fish dry flies we gravitate toward the grotesque. The latest rage is topwater fishing for silver salmon. The fly du jour is a large, winged wad of fluorescent pink deer hair. It's called the Pollywog, although it looks more like a radioactive fruit bat.

Admittedly these are all attractor patterns, and I'm sure that, decades ago, some of the fussier fly throwers of the day wondered exactly what the inventors of the Mickey Finn and the Parmachene Belle were burning in their pipes. But in Alaska, even when we set out to imitate something specific it gets ugly quick, because there is nothing delicate about our trouts' diets. Our idea of a "natural" dry fly is the Deer Hair Mouse, or vole, or shrew (it's a blessing we haven't any woodchucks). And while it's true you may notice the odd trillion insects buzzing around your head as you fish here, our fatso rainbows don't bother sipping low calorie no-seeums off the surface when the bottom is littered with nice juicy salmon eggs.

Imitating those little protein orbs has led to an angling technique that resembles fly fishing only in the tackle it uses to get the hook into the river. Glo Bugs, Iliamna Pinkies, and, lately, an assortment of plastic beads are arguably the most effective and least aesthetic trout baits since canned corn, marshmallows, and cheese balls. But leave it to Alaskans to lower our already abysmal standards with the introduction of the "pegged" bead, the lodge guides' secret weapon for pleasing number-crunching sports who have paid obscene amounts of money to be flown out to remote rivers and really need to catch lots of fish.

I'm not going to explain exactly how the pegged bead works—in part because it is illegal on many of our blue ribbon "fly-fishing only" rivers, but mostly because it is so deadly you would have to try it anyway. Let me just say that a problem with plastic beads is that while they look exactly like salmon eggs, unlike roe they are rock hard, so a trout may mouth nearly every one you drift near him, yet spit them out faster than you can calculate your guide's tip. But a "pegged" bead is virtually impossible for a trout to spit without getting the hook in his face, no matter how quick he is. It's "Fish on!" all day long.

Is it effective? Beyond your wildest dreams. Is it fly fishing? In Alaska it is.

Though these tactics may sound like incredibly bad form, in all fairness to pegged bead devotees, a trout foul-hooked on the outside of the mandible is probably less prone to injury than one that has inhaled a realistic baitfish pattern. Still, the use of some of these Alaskan patterns, and particularly beads, while elevating catch rates, has culled much of the skill, the finesse, and, some might argue, the fun, from both fly tying and fly fishing. A popular outdoor writer, defending the practice in the *Anchorage Daily News*, said, "Any idiot with a spinning rod can catch fish on beads." And he was defending it against my putatively "purist" complaints that the practice is entirely unsportsmanlike.

I have no desire to go back to the Fan Wing Royal Coachman dressed with homemade paraffin and gasoline floatant, any more than I want to trade my toasty Gore-Tex and neoprene waders in for rubber hip boots, or my graphite rods for that Fenwick fiberglass club I started out with forty years ago. But you can whip up a half-dozen Coho Flies or Alaskabous in the time it takes to tie one decent Prince Nymph, and there is actually a little tool that extrudes perfectly spherical Glo Bugs. And, let's face it, it's almost impossible to fish a Bunny Bug incorrectly. Then there are the pegged beads, which will hook fish while even the most reflex-challenged angler is busy gazing up at the clouds pondering life's great mysteries, such as the presence of Canadian bacon on a Hawaiian-style pizza, for instance.

The fact is, here in Alaska, I've actually seen a bait fisherman (apparently overcome with nostalgia, or possibly Coleman fumes) carrying his cured salmon roe bait on his hip in a beautiful old wicker creel. You really do have to go way out of your way to offend anyone's sense of tradition—or even find one. When the spawned-out salmon carcasses begin to rot in our rivers and everyone is using "flesh" flies, you're considered a bit of a snob if you fish a maggot pattern.

And we don't limit our blasphemies to pattern selection. We do things to presentation that would put the guys down at the Catskill Fly Fishing Center and Museum into therapy. Any day during the sockeye run, you will find several hundred, possibly several thousand, anglers at the Kenai/Russian River confluence, a designated "Fly Fishing Only" area, standing, quite literally elbow to elbow, plunking #2 Coho Flies weighted with rubber-core sinkers the size of your baby finger. As long as the sinker is attached at least eighteen inches above the hook, the Alaska Department of Fish and Game decrees that this is indeed fly fishing—not that anybody would mistake it for fly *casting*. With that much lead on, you're not going to attempt a back cast, of course, because you would either snap the tip of your rod or kill someone in the crowd standing behind you waiting for your slot in the meat line. In fact, smart anglers eschew bulky fly line altogether in favor of straight mono. The fly is delivered in a short flip a few yards upstream from your position; then as it sinks, you follow it with the tip of the rod until it begins to rise toward the surface at the end of the drift. At that moment, you give your rod a hopeful and hefty yank (in case a salmon has foolishly ventured near the point of the hook) and flip the heavy rig back upstream again. You do that over and over and over, all day and all night, if necessary, until you've beached your three-salmon limit. Of course, this only works if the guys snugged up against your elbows on either side of you coordinate their sinker flips with yours. When things are going well and there aren't too many rookies in the mix, an entire stretch of the riverbank will become a kind of undulating ballet of rod tips rhythmically rising and falling in unison, their steel line guides glinting in the afternoon sun. As fly fishing goes, it's as close to beauty as we get up here. I swear it can bring a tear to your eye.

Realistically, it's the only effective way to catch sockeye in that particular piece of water, and their oily red flesh, pan fried in butter with garlic and a little dill, justifies almost anything. Even so, Alaskans' perverse corruption of the sport cannot be explained entirely in terms of food-gathering pragmatism. A guy I know from Anchorage, an educated and otherwise civilized person who actually grew up on the classic small streams of Pennsylvania, fishes the catch and release steelhead river behind my house using a gorgeous split bamboo rod. I could describe the soft caramel coloring of the cane, the fine silk wraps. But the salient detail is the way he rigs it with a long leader of 12-lb test Maxima, two or three split shots the size of gumballs, and a hank of pink Glo Bug yarn cinched into the knot at the eye of an enormous, otherwise bare hook. "Barbaric," you snort? Maybe. But in some other, far better life, you might catch half as many steelhead as that guy does.

To the purist all this must sound like some newly discovered circle of hell: a place swarming with huge trout and salmon and no respectable way for a person of refinement to catch them. Here's what I recommend: Slip into that tweed walking jacket and fire up your meerschaum; clamp a fine wire dry fly hook in your vise. Carefully tie in several stiff fibers from a high-quality medium dun hackle feather for the tail, then a stripped peacock quill for the body; add two perfectly matched barred wood duck wings, and another medium dun for the hackle itself. It's beautiful, isn't it? A classic Quill Gordon, almost complete.

But wait. Before you whipfinish the head, tie in two wraps of the hottest, flaming pink chenille you can find (don't worry if you smash the hackle or the wings).

Now, knot the fly to your tippet, clamp at least three large split shot eighteen inches above it, and fish the damned thing right on the bottom.

You may be in Alaska, but that whirring sound you hear is coming all the way from the grave of Theodore Gordon.

Chapter 8

The Last Fish

Here on the Kenai Peninsula in Southcentral Alaska, the legal fishing season on our local rivers runs from Memorial Day to New Year's Eve. There is a nice symmetry to that: the last day of the season falling on the last day of the year. At these latitudes, however, that closing date is only nominal—most years, the rivers are running with slush, if not frozen solid, by Halloween. Anyone out looking for open water on New Year's Eve is either drunk or crazy. Or both.

Today is the second of December. At sunrise (which came a few minutes before ten this morning) the thermometer read a neat round zero. It is snowing steadily, as it has been for weeks. The river has been more or less frozen for the past month. The driveway could pass for a low budget ski slope, and in our woodstove we are burning beetle-killed spruce by the armloads. The nuthatches and our resident woodpecker have fled south to Kodiak or maybe even Sitka, leaving the bird feeder to the intrepid boreal chickadees—the only creatures, beside ravens, who are capable of fleeing Alaska, but are either too obstinate or just stupid enough to stay here all winter. Not counting us.

We lost three minutes and forty-six seconds of daylight today and we are not going to get them back until next summer. These are the weeks of the long nights. At the Save-U-More there is a vodka bottle in many a shopping cart. Around town, the sales of full spectrum lighting units, aromatherapy supplies, yoga classes, and DVD rentals are way up. The next several months are going to get rough, and I know it. I've been through it twenty-eight times before. When the fly shop catalogs arrive in the mail now I can't even look at the photos of fishermen wading sun-drenched bonefish flats in their swimsuits.

My wife and I and our four cats live approximately two hundred miles south of Anchorage, on the Anchor River, a few miles upstream from the clear river's termination with the saltwater of Cook Inlet. Late this afternoon, in what passes for relief from the drudgery of winter around here, I drove into the nearby town of Anchor Point to take the garbage and recycling to the dumpsters at the transfer station, and to pick up the mail at the post office. As I said, it's a very long winter.

I thought *I* had it bad until this afternoon. I'm apparently not the only one. Coming back across the old steel trestle bridge over the Anchor River shortly after the 3:52 p.m. official sunset, I spied a guy in a snowmobile suit and bunny boots standing on the river ice, plunking a line into a narrow lead of fast-moving open water running the length of the big pool below the bridge, known by fishermen as the Bridge Hole of course.

The ambient temperature was maybe fifteen degrees. The residual daylight, meager as it is at this time of year, was further dimmed with brooding snow-laden clouds. There was already a foot of fresh snow on the ice, marked by the loopy meandering trail of a local moose that had clearly been browsing the bank willows, and also by the straighter, more purposeful tracks of the fisherman: a double line of boot prints which ran directly from the one car in the parking lot to the back of his heels. Downstream a hundred feet, the black seam of open water vanished beneath a massive ice jam heaped upon the boulder garden at the tailout of the pool. If this crazy bastard went into the drink, it was going to take dynamite to find his body. Here, I said to myself, is a man who either really loves his steelhead fishing or has started in on the holiday drinking a little early. Or both.

I pulled into the parking lot below the bridge next to a rusted AMC Hornet in which a woman sat reading a paperback under the dome light, exhaust billowing out from somewhere under the car where a tailpipe once existed. It's a sure sign of winter solstice in Alaska when a woman would rather sit in the parking lot of a fishing hole risking carbon monoxide poisoning than spend another minute in the cabin.

Heater running, I sat in my truck and watched the man fish for a short time, wondering how he planned to release any steelhead he might hook without crawling to the very edge of the ice to do so. But I also found myself thinking about opening day of the fishing season on our river, the last weekend of May—six very long, very cold, very dark months out there in front of us. If the man had so much as rolled a fish, I would have been on my way home for my fly vest and thermal undies.

The Anchor River empties into the salt of Cook Inlet at Anchor Point, the westernmost point on the contiguous highway system of North America. A mile and a half upriver from the beach is the steel trestle bridge spanning the river in the town of Anchor Point where I witnessed that lonely but intrepid winter solstice fisherman out there at the edge of the ice, casting into the Bridge Hole.

The Bridge Hole is a much busier place in the summertime, and for good reason. It features a big gravel parking lot, picnic tables, and a modern concrete outhouse. There is a little steel box mounted on a post for the five-dollar daily use fee. Across the road to the beach, there used to be a tackle shop and a huge fish-weighing scale where many silver or king salmon made their official entry into the summer derby held there. Within walking distance of the fishing hole is the bar and restaurant at the Anchor River Inn, offering all the things a man could want after a hard day's fishing: food, drinks, pool tables, and a huge big-screen TV.

The Bridge Hole itself is a deep, straight trough with a high cutbank and a forest of cottonwoods on the north side and a long, easy-to-wade gravel bar on the south shore. It is also the first good water anglers come upon after making the four-hour drive from the big city of Anchorage. With a tackle shop on one bank and a bar on the other, it is obviously going to be the hardest fished hole on the river. During the first salmon run of the season, in May and June, fishing is allowed only downstream from the bridge to protect the spawning king salmon upriver.

The crowds at the Bridge Hole can get pretty dense as anglers jam as close as they can get to the Alaska Department of Fish and Game's NO FISHING ABOVE THIS POINT signs on both sides of the river. For this reason, it is not my favorite place to fish, although I've braved the mobs on occasion in order to put the first fresh salmon fillets of the year on the Memorial Day grill. Later in the summer, when the upper river opens to fishing for steelhead and trout, I am happiest walking the mostly unfished water behind the house that my wife and I built on a promontory overlooking the Anchor River valley a few miles upstream from the bridge.

As is the tradition on trout streams everywhere, favorite fishing holes on the Anchor River have names given them by their devotees. Even the Alaska State Parks Department recognizes the legitimacy of such longstanding monikers. Each of the parking areas and camping sites along the heavily fished section between the Bridge Hole and the ocean have official signs reading Picnic Hole, Dudas Hole (named after a local family), and Slide Hole. Below the Slide Hole is the less officially named Grass Hole located at the peak of the high tide mark where tall salt grasses line the twice-daily flooded mud banks. On the upper river, one hole is known as Dolly Land. I would love to say that it is the favorite fishing hole of that great country music star herself. But in truth it was named for the numerous small Dolly Varden char it attracts each summer and fall. It is right behind my house.

Dolly Land is a long walk from the public access at the bridge. But from my back door it is about an eight-minute hike down a steep ravine filled with blown-down spruce and then across a couple hundred yards of knee-deep bog. When I started building the house in the late 1980s it was also one of the best steelhead holes on the river and anglers often did hike the two miles upstream from the bridge just to fish Dolly Land. It was that good. But like all rivers it has changed, and not for the better, and very few people make the long walk to fish the less productive water any longer.

My wife, Lin, and I bought the three acres our house now sits on in 1983, shortly after we moved to Alaska from the Lower 48. Although we lived and worked in the big city of Anchorage, two hundred miles north of the property, over the next twenty years we built on it almost continuously: first a tent platform, then a small cabin, and finally a real house on the edge of the ridge above Dolly Land. With the exceptions of a concrete contractor and an electrician, and the help of several loyal friends from time to time, Lin and I built much of the place by hand ourselves, working through summer vacations and more weekends than I care to think about now, making the four-hour drive each way to and from Anchorage, our pickup truck stuffed with building materials and tools. It is a very slow way to build a house.

Finally, in the summer of 2002 we moved down here to the river full time, and I got ready to settle in and enjoy my lifetime dream of living on a wild steelhead stream. I pictured myself fishing Dolly Land every day during the great fall runs of anadromous fish, the peppy little dollies and the big beautiful steelhead just waiting to be fooled by a fly—right there in my backyard!

However, our very first autumn on the river we were hammered with the "one-hundred-year" flood of October 2002.

Monsoon-like rains drenched the southern Kenai Peninsula for a week, raising the Anchor River far above flood levels to near historic highs. At the bridge, the river came up over the banks and tore out the parking lot; the road to the beach had to be closed. On nearby rivers the highway bridges washed out, briefly disconnecting the town of Anchor Point from the rest of the world. Obviously, my plans for bucolic fall fishing in my backyard got put on hold. The flood waters were so powerful that Dolly Land actually moved more than a hundred feet out of its normal channel, the river carving a new run into the woods along what had been its south bank.

"Oh well," I said, patiently, as the river crested and the roads closed. "Mother Nature, and all that. What are you gonna do?"

You can't help but get philosophical about a hundred-year flood, seeing how it is, after all, a once in a lifetime event. However, when the second one-hundred-year flood came three weeks later in November, I watched from our living room window, incredulous and far less amused as the river valley filled and became a lake. The tops of the naked cottonwood trees protruded from the muddy, rain-splattered surface like the beseeching hands of thousands of drowning victims. Somewhere at the bottom of that lake was my already damaged Dolly Land, or whatever was left of it, as it took its second beating in one month. Needless to say, I did not get a lot of fishing in that first season.

I have to admit I started to take it personally. For twenty years I had been building a house within a short walk of one of the best steelhead holes on one of the very few unspoiled, undammed rivers full of entirely wild steelhead left on American soil. I'm a rather pessimistic mope by nature, a trait that has served me well—though it hasn't made me easy to live with. The beauty of pessimism is that you can only be pleasantly surprised when good things occasionally happen. At the same time, you feel pretty smug when, more frequently, reality is its uncooperative self. But two one-hundred-year floods in six weeks? This was a little over the top. Around Thanksgiving, weeks after the river was finally back to normal for the second time, I hiked down to inspect the damage. I found, in a bed of displaced river sand among the trees in the middle of the forest, a steelhead, high and dry and very dead. I began to think that either Mother Nature was one mean-spirited broad or She had a wacky sense of humor.

In a world full of disasters, this is pretty minor stuff, of course: a few bridges and parking lots washed out, the road destroyed a couple times, lots of cottonwoods turned into easy beaver food. The personal property toll was relatively light: a few people who had places on the banks of the river lost their cabins and the assorted junk cars that we consider yard art in this part of the world. But nobody was seriously hurt in the flooding, and in the face of real suffering—Katrina-style, for example—devoting two decades of my life to building a fishing shack and then losing all the good water is really pretty fluffy as disasters go.

The following summer, when the river opened to fishing behind our house for the first time since the big floods, I once again called upon my pathetically thin stores of hope and optimism and hiked down to Dolly Land, fly rod in hand, hoping that somehow everything would be as before. Dolly Land was actually missing—at least the hole I had known by that name for two decades. At the head of where the pool used to start, there was a smooth, flat-topped boulder where I often sat and tied on a leader and fly or enjoyed a salami sandwich. Sitting in the sunshine on that big boulder, my feet dangling in the shallows, I had more than once sat and congratulated myself on the capture and release of a big steelhead, celebrating with a can of beer from my pack.

But that big flat boulder was now a half-acre of gravel and rocks distant from the new Dolly Land hole. The heart of the old Dolly Land sat high and dry, baking in the afternoon sun, and with it any hopes I had of hanging onto the past. Optimism really is a bad idea.

Already, grasses and crimson-leafed fireweed shoots were unfurling in the soil between the boulders around which I had once drifted my Glo Bugs and streamers. Willows would take hold next, and then alders. And then, over the years, cottonwoods and maybe even a few black spruce would move in, if the ground stayed dry long enough. I knew that rivers changed, that bends oxbowed into sloughs and then into landlocked ponds and then marshes and finally thickets and forests. A history of satellite photos of any small river will verify that. And simply walking across the bottomlands of my own property it was easy to see the long, winding declivities where the old riverbeds lay hidden in the weeds, the old channels gone to bushes and trees over the years. But I always assumed that such natural progressions were the products of history in all its famous sluggishness—not the aftermath of sudden events. Stunned by the river's dramatic upheaval, I walked across the huge barren gravel bar that had been the bottom of my favorite fishing hole. I stood on the bank of the new channel, taking no pleasure in the fact that Dolly Land was now a hundred feet closer to my house than it had been a year before.

The new cutbank, across from where I stood, had been gouged out of the forest ten months prior to this, but was still slowly crumbling into the water in places, the river apparently still testing the possibilities of further incursion into the land mass. Large planes of the forest floor, undercut by the flood, had fissured and caved away from the bank, and now slanted down into the water—trees and all. A dozen cottonwood sweepers, barely anchored by what was left of their roots, lay crisscrossed over each other on the surface of the river, bobbing rhythmically in the current. Heaped at the tail end of the run, there was a huge jumble of downed trees, fresh with new summer leaves, a shocking green in the tannic river water, like strange freshwater kelp.

But aside from those downed trees, there was a disturbing lack of life. Nothing moved in the water or on the surface. If the big schools of Dollies had been there as usual, it would have been easy to see them flashing as they gorged on caddis casings in the shallows. It was summer and the king salmon should have been evident: deep red torpedoes fringed with fungus, torquing and twisting in their egg-laying, sperm-spuming, life-and-death dance. But there was nothing there in the new river channel. Even the ubiquitous schools of little salmon smolt were missing. And perhaps most frightening of all, the clouds of gnats and midges on which the tiniest fish feasted were also absent. The river bottom had been scraped and scoured by the enormous flood waters, and then smothered under immeasurable tons of silt as the flood subsided. Not even the riparian insects were left alive.

I walked along the strange new river, looking but not finding any fish among nature's wreckage, not finding the insect hatches I should have been seeing, not finding the eagles and yellowlegs and kingfishers and ouzels and mergansers that should have been there, that I had always taken for granted as being there. I was overcome by the dystopian feel haunting what had so recently been a paradise for me. The sickening feeling of seeing nature so badly wounded was one I had not experienced since I was a child living in the industrial wastelands of Western New York State, not far from the infamous Love Canal. And the fact that this time nature had done it to itself was little comfort to me as I stood there in the middle of the destruction.

Wherever I went upstream or down from Dolly Land, it looked like the concussion from a bomb blast had rolled down the river valley. Mature cottonwoods, uprooted and shattered by the raging floodwaters, lay scattered along endless barren gravel bars. At every bend in the river, I found exploded tree trunks and limbs stacked in enormous heaps, two stories high in places. I walked all the way to the bridge and called my wife on the cell phone and asked her to come and get me. I couldn't bear walking all the way back upstream to the house again through the devastation.

Down at the Bridge Hole things were not as gloomy. The deep and heavily bouldered nature of that hole had saved it; that, and the nearly straight path the river followed there in its lower reaches where the fresh water made its final dash to the beach and the sea. That straightness had allowed the flood surge to race through it without changing the shapes of the banks significantly and without depositing the silt it carried. In the woods on the north bank of the Bridge Hole, there was weedy debris dangling from the cottonwoods high above the ground at the line of the flood's highest point. But there was nothing like the damage I had seen in the upper river behind my house where the water had cut across the meadows and tundra, picking up silt and mud and whole living trees, and then dropping its messy load again as it was slowed by the next serpentine bend. No, the Bridge Hole looked pretty good. I was going to have to fish with the crowds for a while.

Nature being nature, and having infinite time to deal with things, even Dolly Land finally made a gradual comeback. Over the next few summers, the dark brown caddis flies and little gray mayflies and the almost invisible midges began showing up in the riffles again at the upper end of the run, and the Dollies and the salmon smolt—who somehow miraculously hatched through the silted river bottom—appeared once more to feed on them. Five years later, after the mostly forgotten, twin one-hundred-year floods of 2002, I was back at Dolly Land when it opened to fishing that summer. And the fishing was good. I was happy to find that a skated elk hair caddis or a floating emerger brought lots of strikes from the smaller fish that were schooling there once again. The steelhead fishing improved too. That fall there were some nice fish holding again in the heart of the new Dolly Land where the water had finally scoured away the excess silt. I guess that if you live long enough, you'll see just about everything—bad and good.

By this time, we had almost finished the house construction at last—though the project was at that stage where the house was standing, with walls and a roof and doors and windows and plumbing and electric lights, and looked mostly complete to anyone but the guy building it—or his wife. I could put in whole days of work, finishing window casings and exterior trim moldings and the endless taping and sanding and painting that it takes to finish the interior of a house, and at the end of the day no one but Lin and I could identify what I had done all day that so exhausted me. I had to finish the house. But I also had to go fishing.

With October, autumn came fast and so did the rains. A series of huge low pressure systems moved up from the Gulf of Alaska in a steady chain of storms that caused the river to blow out nearly every week. For days, I worked inside, listening to each new downpour pelting the metal roof. I watched rain sheet down the windows as I built covers for the baseboard heating elements in the sunroom. It was a good time to get some work done and a bad time for fishing anyway, I told myself—even if it was the peak of the steelhead run. The river was high and muddy and unfishable. I sawed and hammered and screwed and glued, and sanded and painted and sanded and painted some more.

As I may have mentioned, I'm easily depressed and I'll admit that I respond rather simplistically to the weather. A couple weeks of rain can flatten me. But I like to work with tools at least as much as I like to fish, and so as long as I stayed busy, I was able to tell myself that the rain would end one day and I would fish again that year—if the river did not actually flood again. Everyone who had been around in 2002 started twitching. There was a horribly familiar relentlessness to this rain. I drove into town daily, supposedly to get the mail or throw the trash or the recycling. But it was no coincidence I had to cross the bridge and look at the muddy waters rising each time I made that trip. There were no cars in the parking lot, no one fishing the raging river. Not even a steelhead fisherman would be crazy enough for that. I finished the sunroom and turned my attention to the railing on the loft, trying not to think about what was going on outside. I had seen the river destroyed once by capricious Mother Nature, and I did not want to wait another three or four years for Dolly Land to recuperate again.

One day in mid-October the rain trickled to a stop, the meager fall sun peeked out, the temperature dropped, and it became true autumn in Alaska: cold and clear and beautiful, and very short-lived. The rainstorm winds had stripped the last of the yellow-brown leaves off the cottonwoods. And when the clouds finally drifted away completely, I could see the Caribou Hills just to the south of us, home of the headwaters of the Anchor River. The hills were covered in snow. Winter was nearly upon us.

I had wasted precious October steelhead days working indoors on projects I could have nibbled away at all winter long. Now, just as the last chance to fish before the river froze up was here, I needed to finish the exterior siding and the decks and stairs on the porch, work on the roof flashings that absolutely had to be finished—jobs that really can't be managed in the snow and darkness that was coming. I went back to work outside, trying to cram in the last exterior projects before the work season ended as surely as the fishing season was about to.

The nights were brittle with cold, the temps dropping into the twenties. The river levels fell rapidly as the ponds and bogs and tributaries in the hills locked up with ice. Mornings I bundled up and worked with gloves on, the compressor sometimes frosting up in the cold air. Just as the river was getting down to fishable levels, it also began to freeze. Finally, when I got caught up with the exterior projects, when the house was dry and tight and secure against the weather to the point that nothing was going to get wet or freeze or be otherwise ruined by winter in a way that would obviously look like a failure of my handiwork, I went fishing.

Bundled up in the wool and Gore-Tex that steelheaders everywhere don, I clambered down the icy ravine and across the frozen bog to Dolly Land one cold and cloudy morning instead of hauling my tools out of the garage. The river was thick with slush. I could not even get a split shot through it. I made a couple casts in the cold light of the mid-morning dawn, and packed it in when the first snowflakes began to flutter down onto the river. I climbed the slippery trail back to the house, peeled off my waders and went back to work with the tools.

Over the last two weeks of October, the weather got better, warmer. But each time it warmed up, the tributaries thawed and the river rose and went off-color. I made the same backbreaking trip to Dolly Land through the fallen, beetle-killed spruce in the ravine and across the boot-sucking mud in the bog and then back up the steep ridge to my house again, several more times. But it became less and less appealing each time I arrived at the river only to find it high and muddied. By the end of the month I had caught just a handful of steelhead behind the house, and was wearying of the death march each trip had become—not to mention the feeling that those mostly fishless trips were taking a lot of precious time out of the work that needed to be done on the house before winter.

We've all heard the clever cliché about how on the day we die we will not wish we had worked more and fished less. That may be true. But if the roof flashing did not get finished and caulked before it was buried in two feet of snow, my wife and I were going to wake up one morning during a January warm spell with snowmelt dripping on our faces. I don't know anyone who would want to extend his life in those circumstances.

So, toward the end of the season, with winter looming over my last uncompleted outdoor project, when the call of the river was too much to resist, I would lay down my tools and drive to the bridge instead of making the difficult march down to my beloved Dolly Land. Thus, I was at the Bridge Hole when I caught my last fish of the season this year. It was the first week of November, a month ago now. Nightly temperatures were down in the teens and the shelf ice was extending its death grip across the shallows from both shores beneath the bridge. There was still about twenty feet of open water right down the middle of the river, however. If you got the timing just right, there were fish to be had. Mornings, the river was full of slush and clumps of floating ice so thick there was not enough split shot in the world to sink a fly through it. I took to working around the house until the midday temps hovered near the forty-degree mark—usually about three in the afternoon—promising open water. Then I would suit up and race to the Bridge Hole and join the half-dozen other graybeards who make up the midweek, midday contingent of guys who have the leisure to fish when younger, more industrious men are working.

I took a spot near the top end of the Bridge Hole. For days the action had been concentrated near the tailout. Therefore, the regulars were arriving early to nail down that stretch of water. I thought ruefully that I should have come earlier, but the idea of putting on enough lead to crash through the slush for an hour just to be in position when the river melted sounded a little too calculated to fall under the heading of fun. Maybe living on a river for a while rids you of the need to fish every minute in exactly the right place. Never mind the thought of how cold my feet would have been by the time the river thawed.

I tied on a Glo Bug, the standard steelhead and dolly fly for the Anchor at this time of year. It is a boring, unimpressive fly, but really, this late in the season my urge to experiment had worn a little thin and there was only an hour or two of fishing time before the sun set and the river slushed up again. Weighted with three medium split shot, I hurled the awkward rig into the slot, wanting, of course, one more fish to end the year, because it was clear that these days were coming to a close. It was a dreary end to a fishing season: standing under the bridge with a bunch of guys across from the shuttered tackle shop, lethargically plunking a hunk of yarn and dragging lead across the bottom of the river. But it is an easy walk from the parking lot to the river, and this was as close to fishing as

I was going to get for months to come, and I have to admit it felt pretty good.

Below me a short distance was a guy named Mike, one of the regulars. An old-timer on the Anchor River. He had a pointy white beard and wore a tall, funny-looking watch cap every single day of the fishing season. In the spring, he fished the low tide in the salt chuck for king salmon, and in mid-summer when the silvers showed up he and his hat might be seen anywhere in the lower river. But late in the season, he practically moved into the Bridge Hole and stayed there until the last steelhead was pulled through the last sliver of open water on the day the river ice finally slammed shut for good. I drove across that bridge each day fetching the mail, and Mike and his funny hat had been standing in that same place for two weeks, casting into the same run for as long as the water remained ice free. He had been doing that for years.

They say go with what you know. Mike clearly knew something I didn't; he was catching one Dolly after another. It seemed like he landed ten on ten consecutive casts. Dollies are a school fish, sometimes clustering together like a bunch of grapes in a little dip in the river bottom. I figured he had a batch pinned down, had figured out the drift, and was rolling his Glo Bug right into them. I shrugged. *Let him mess around with those little Dollies*, I told myself. I was there to catch one last steelhead. Besides, it was not the first time I was within casting distance of a guy who was outfishing me and making it look easy. Humility is a virtue, right? Well, I can use all the extra virtue anyone was giving away. I cast and cast and caught nothing.

I changed to a different colored Glo Bug. Nothing. I added weight, took weight off. Nothing. In a while, it became clear that no one was catching any steelhead—not even the deadly Mike—and so I took off the big steelhead bug and tried fishing with small nymphs, figuring I'd end the year with a few Dollies at any rate; they can rarely resist a hare's ear nymph or a caddis larva imitation. Nothing.

Mike, standing fifteen feet away from me, caught about six more fish in the time it took me to change flies three times. He was a hell of a fisherman and he deserved every fish he caught. He had put in years learning every rock and every current in this hole—which, as I said, had not been changed much by the floods—and now he was reaping the benefits of his experience.

I'd seen his type on every river I ever fished: those rock-steady, fish-slaying guys who stand in one place doing whatever works and nothing else, saying nothing to anyone. They are as inscrutable as professional Hold 'em champs, enigmas to me. They devote a lot of time to something they seem to take little pleasure from. Fishing is sometimes called a sport, a word defined as "an activity involving physical exertion and skill in which an individual or a team competes against another for entertainment." There is a notation in my dictionary that a "dated" use of that word is *fun.* As in "it was great sport to tease him." Obviously, the Mikes of the world with their enviable skills are sticking to the primary definition. I have not decided whether they are blessed with unlimited patience or cursed with a total lack of imagination. Or both.

I kept changing flies and catching nothing, drifting into a bit of a trance, wondering about how much of a sport fishing really was. That led me to wonder if I should maybe pull up and go home and do something truly constructive—such as constructing a door for the woodshed before the horizontal winds of winter filled it with wet, firewood-drenching snow. Stuff like that.

I was yanked out of my thoughts when Mike let out a yelp. I glanced over to see that, apparently while releasing yet another fish, he had put the hook through the back of his hand. So I waded downstream to where he was positioned, where he had been positioned for most of the summer. Although it was true that I had trudged over to help a fellow angler in need, it really was a great excuse to find out what he was using. And, of course, what he was using was a pegged bead. It was astounding to me that a local guy like Mike, who could practically talk to the fish in our river—a fish assassin who killed an annual limit of five king salmon every year and took home more silvers using a fly rod than most dipnetters caught in a season—needed to stoop to such a low tactic as the pegged bead.

Mike was embarrassed to admit that he had indeed resorted to pegging, a legalized form of snagging detested by all but the most callous, fish-grubbing anglers. But, as I mashed the barb off the point of his hook with my pliers and pulled it out of the back of his hand, he told me he had tried every fly in his box and had finally given up earlier that week when it became clear that the dollies would not touch anything but a bead. The steelhead, he added, would not touch anything at all at these temperatures. He declared that if he was going to stand out there in water turning to slush around his knees, then, by God, he was going to catch fish, and that this late hour of the season was not the time for screwing around with sporting ethics or finesse, or anything that resembled fair play. He rubbed the hole in the back of his hand and looked up at the ominous clouds, threatening snow. "We don't have much time left," he said.

Even setting aside the question of why a person would feel so obliged to stand in freezing water to catch and then release fish in the first place, Mike's argument eluded me. We feel compelled to do whatever it takes (no matter how low) to catch fish that we don't want to keep anyway—even if we are embarrassed by what we do to catch them? Try explaining that kind of desperation to someone who does not fish.

It was not the first time I had been mystified by the reasoning of another angler. I shrugged and grunted in agreement with him, and then went back to my slot. I took two more casts, thinking about his argument, and realized that he was absolutely and categorically wrong about everything; everything except the fact that—barring an unprecedented heat wave before the end of the month—this was probably going to be the last time I fished the river this year.

The shelf ice was pushing farther out every day, and the hours of open water were decreasing just as quickly. I had to go out of town the following week, and by the time I got back it would be over for another season. That meant six long, cold months without a fly rod in my hand. I still had one last half-hour of daylight and open water. Did I want to borrow a plastic bead from Mike and peg a bare Gamakatsu hook below it a couple inches so that I snagged the poor stupid dollies in the side of the mouth when they made the mistake of touching that little store-bought egg imitation? Did I want one last fish that badly? It was a good question.

I snipped off the useless nymph I had been using and looked in my fly box. Among the hideous pink and chartreuse and magenta and cerise marabou and yarn and tinsel and flashabou monstrosities lying in it, was one old Spruce Fly. The simple chicken feather and silk floss fly looked dull and sad, stuck there in the midst of all that tinsel like a retired elementary school principal at a Gary Glitter concert. I had actually tied it several years ago for a trip to the Rockies and some Madison River browns. But thinking back to a time, a quarter century before, when I first started tying steelhead flies, it occurred to me that the Spruce Fly was one of those old venerable patterns like the Skykomish Sunrise and the Silver Hilton that I had long since eschewed in favor of the harem of hot pink floozies that fill my box today.

Deciding to go out in style, I put on a sink tip and I tied on the old fly. I laid it out onto the river, and it felt so good to cast without lead. The repetitive plunking of the Glo Bug and split shots had become such a part of my life I almost forgot how pleasant and fluid it felt to make a cast that actually rolled over in a curve instead of falling out of the sky like a doomed asteroid.

I swung the old streamer through the Bridge Hole, letting it hang at the end of the drift, almost in front of Mike's knees, feeling the river gripping it like a handshake. I had absolutely no confidence in the Spruce Fly, having never caught anything on that pattern—or, for that matter, on any of the old steelhead classics. *But*, I thought, *at least I ended the season feeling like I was fly fishing for a change*. And then on the second or third cast, the fish hit and I have never been more completely surprised by a strike in my life. I really thought I must have foul-hooked it. It was a steelhead, a small one, about six pounds or so. It was cold and sluggish, and I horsed it in on the heavy tippet and found the old fly neatly planted inside its upper lip, as pretty a hookup as you could ask for. Without taking it out of the icy water, I let the fish loose and called it a day. And a season.

A few days before this, I had opened the mail to find among the various ads and credit card offers, a small postcard urging me to subscribe to a certain outdoor magazine. The copy made the following assertion:

> "There are three stages in the life of a sportsman: 1) The early phase in which you just want to catch or shoot stuff, lots of stuff. 2) The technical phase in which you become fascinated with the gear. And 3) The enlightened phase in which how much you shoot or catch, or even what you get, is not as important as the way you do it."

This, I assumed, was the highest level to attain. This was where the sport lay—according to the ad guys who wrote this kind of stuff.

It is a lovely, sentimental theory, and I dismissed it as such. After twenty-five years in Alaska I have seen nothing but a steady cancer-like growth in the first stage of that idealized model. Everything is about numbers; size and quantity rule above all other measurements of a day's fishing. Spend a few minutes in an Alaskan fly shop and you will hear so many figures rattled off you'll think you are at a retirement seminar. Maybe it's like that all over, but at least on some of the Lower 48 rivers there are vestiges of the fussy old sporting ethics that temper our lust for prodigious numbers of fish. Sure, those traditions are sometimes laughable. Even so, a little enlightenment can't hurt.

In my own way, I'm just as bad. I pride myself on the fact that I don't care to count and measure every fish I catch. But I will stoop pretty low to put a hook into them. Not as low as a pegged bead maybe, but Glo Bugs lobbed with grapeshot-sized lead? You bet. Monstrous hot pink streamers that look like glam rock costumes? Got boxes of them. Strike indicators that are nothing but sophisticated sounding bobbers? Count me in. I'm no saint, although after that Spruce Fly stunt I was thinking of checking the Vatican website for an application.

Enlightened or otherwise, when I let that fish go and clipped off that fly and turned for the ice covered bank and my truck and home and all the unfinished carpentry waiting for me there, I hoped that I had just earned some points with Mother Nature, or the river gods, or whoever it is that is in charge of hundred-year floods. I prayed that they would keep and protect my beloved Dolly Land through another season or two. And for a couple minutes there, I have to say I almost understood what those romantic fly-fishing magazine writers were talking about.

Either I'm getting soft in the head or just plain old.

Maybe both.

Epilogue: The man I helped get the hook out of his hand was named Mike Anderson. I know that only because the year after I wrote this piece, when the first king salmon started showing up in May, Mike's familiar figure was missing on the Anchor River. When I mentioned his absence to one of the other regulars, he told me that Mike had died earlier that spring, a few weeks before the season opened.

As you might expect, one of the better fishing spots on the lower Anchor River is now known as the Mike Anderson Hole.

Chapter 9

It Takes a Thief

Everyone knows you can't trust anything a fisherman says, especially a fisherman who writes. And obviously, poets are the worst. So it should really come as no big surprise that in a vain attempt to write poetry, I also became a thief.

I am not a serious poet—let me say that up front. Never will be. I have not done the homework, put in the time, or paid the dues. And I just don't drink enough. I probably don't have the ear for it in any case. I'm a simple prose writer, and to prose writers, poetry is all things sophisticated and adult: big game hunting to our frog gigging, tarpon fishing to our panfish trips. Nothing to fool around with. It's The Show. I know all this. But it's like being forbidden to play with your big brother's chemistry set. Who can resist whipping up a surreptitious beaker of something that bubbles and fizzes, even if it stinks, too? So I always have one or more poems under way. They're exercises I do when I don't have time to write longer pieces. And if I'd only remembered that these poems were just that, *exercises*, everything would have been fine.

Sometimes, some aspect of fishing begs to be written succinctly, and only a poem can capture it. A couple years ago I wrote one considering the absurdity of catch-and-release fly fishing. It's always dicey to start questioning things that are essential to your self-image, particularly in the middle of a poem, in the middle of the night. But isn't that just the sort of thing real poets do? I wanted to think so. I poured myself some Irish whiskey and pursued the idea, and the result was something that I thought looked pretty respectable for a dabbler. Maybe it was the whiskey.

In any case, I sent it out, and was pleased when it appeared in *Gray's Sporting Journal* in 2003, and more than happy to cash the one-hundred-dollar check that came in the mail with my copies. Every aspiring poet wants to announce that he or she is a published poet; I was now a *paid* poet. But even through the fog of satisfaction, I could see that something was wrong with the poem. It was just a little too familiar. Not to mention, a little too smart.

That's when I thought of the poet Billy Collins.

As dread spread through me, I pulled Collins's 1999 collection *Questions About Angels* off my shelf and turned to the poem "Forgetfulness." I had forgotten that I'd read it. And then I had burglarized it.

I'd always liked that poem. And yet, despite its warnings about memory loss, more of it had clung to me than I'd realized. A year or so after I read it, I sent this to *Gray's*:

Some Days I Don't Think
There are some days I don't think
I can catch another fish only to release it.
Was it Nietzsche or Kierkegaard who felt
that the pointlessness of life was the point?
Or was that the Buddha?
Like so many things I once netted
with the tight mesh of my young mind
the philosophers have slipped away now.
Anymore, I don't know the date men died at Hastings.
I'm not sure if Gaul still has three parts.

And using my high school German today
I can order coffee (mit milch und zucker)
—but nothing to go with it.
What I do remember is the last steelhead
last season, the color of the fly,
the weight of the leader, the arc of the drift.
I remember where the fish lay in the pool,
the tug, the frothy eruption,
the time of day, the milky autumn sky.
The leaves were rotting, the salmon rotted.
And I apologize to Proust (I think)
for cherishing the pungent remnants
of a summer packed and gone then
to that retirement home for old summers
which we call memory.
As I said, there are some days I don't think
I can possibly stand to catch one more fish
only to release it.
But, clearly, this is not one of them.

The theme of forgetfulness is close enough to regret having done, but also general enough to forgive. But the examples I used are not only painfully similar—the academic landmarks—but also more pretentious, a sure sign of a writer out of his depth. I wouldn't drop Nietzsche's name in a short story if you held a gun to my head. Then there's Collins's line "memories you used to harbor/decide to retire to the southern hemisphere of the brain," and my "retirement home for old summers/ which we call memory." There's no denying that one. It's like getting caught trying to pawn swag from a heist. Yet remembering the sheer pleasure of those words rolling off my ballpoint, I would have sworn they were my original idea.

My old friend and fishing partner Will Rice recently told me he'd thought he'd created a new mantis shrimp pattern that bonefish could not keep their lips off. He knew he was incorporating features of both Peterson's Spawning Shrimp and the Veverka's Mantis Shrimp patterns. But he was sure his added innovation using synthetic "brush" wire for the body made it something original enough to take credit for. He almost sent it out to one of the big fly producers when he realized his efforts at originality had replicated Enrico Puglisi's E.P. Shrimp.

All of which reminds me that Donald Rumsfeld famously claimed that there are some things "we know we know," some things we know we don't know, and some things "we *don't* know we don't know." What he left out of that is the fact that there are also some things we don't know that we *do* know. Like the existence of other people's poems and fly patterns.

Books are a good example. Reaching a certain age in life, you will have read far more of them than you can possibly remember. The narrators and characters in them come and go in our lives like the people we work and play with. Some of their faces and voices will stick with us forever, yet there are other people we would confidently deny knowing if we were strapped to a polygraph machine and shot full of truth serum. A friend in Anchorage, a voracious reader, once found herself enjoying a book from our independent used bookstore. Halfway through she discovered faintly penciled notes in the margins—in her own handwriting. If you can totally forget a good book, how much of anything we read is sticking? And why some things and not others?

When the reader is also a writer, this phenomenon can be problematic. Nobody would be able to write a word if every syllable triggered a plagiarism alarm. Still, I wish I'd remembered where that line about memory came from before I put my name on it.

We read good stuff because it makes us feel smart. That's one of the things all art does. Logic dictates that writing well should make us feel even smarter. But in trying to carry that cleverness from reading to writing, we are tempted to mimicry. In "The Trouble with Poetry," Collins describes students of poetry, "longing to steal,/ to break into the poems of others/with a flashlight and a ski mask."

I already knew I wasn't a good poet, but my theft, however unintended, was embarrassing. And it was about to get a lot worse.

Aware of my crime now, when I looked at my poem in *Gray's*, the images I stole from Billy Collins were as noticeable and disgusting as dog hairs on a poached egg. But I asked myself: who else will know? How many *Gray's Sporting Journal* readers will have seen or recalled that particular Collins poem? And surely Collins, the most popular poet since Robert Frost, doesn't have time to peruse fishing magazines. Plus, I live in Anchor Point, Alaska—a little off the beaten academic poetry path, to say the least. It was not like I'd ever have to look the guy in the eyes. Besides, it really was an accident. I wrote it off to experience and slept like a baby. A corrupt baby, but a baby still.

A year and a half later, one winter's day, I wandered into the office of Carol Swartz, the director of the Kachemak Bay Campus of the Kenai Peninsula College, in Homer, where I teach part-time. Carol was planning the 2005 Kachemak Bay Writers' Conference, and she told me the good news: Our keynote speaker would be Billy Collins. You cannot make this shit up.

For the next couple months, every time Collins's name came up I slid deeper into a funk of vanity and paranoia, simultaneously wishing and fearing that he not only knew about my obscure crime, but also that he cared. What would he say? I cast to trout and salmon and char on sunny afternoons, indulging myself with fantasies in which Collins declared that I'd actually improved on his poem. But those gave way to middle-of-the-night terrors in which he laughed at my feeble attempt to be something I was not. By the time the conference came around the following June, I was nearly convinced that I should throw myself at his mercy and whimper, "I just wanted to be a poet for a little while."

Billy Collins is a charming, friendly, and genuinely decent guy. The minute I met him at the conference, I knew he would not say anything—even in the absurd off chance he knew about my obscure poem. And that made me want to blurt it out all the more. Luckily, being a coward, I didn't do anything recklessly admirable—like telling him the truth. Besides, Collins was having a great time. Everyone was having a great time. Why dredge up the ugliness? Plagiarism, intellectual dishonesty; who needs that kind of trouble? Furthermore, I was one of the organizers of the conference. I was supposed to be keeping a lid on petty personal dramas, not creating them.

I planned to say nothing, and it looked like I could pull it off—until my wife decided to throw a party for the faculty. I was sure Collins wouldn't show. He was too busy doing every Alaskan thing he could cram into his visit: he'd gone flightseeing over the Augustine Volcano to the Katmai Coast to look at the giant coastal brown bears. He'd been kayaking among the seals. He'd probably be out walking on my favorite beach, noticing things I'd missed but would some day marvel at when I saw them described with originality and deep insights in one of his poems. The only thing he did not do was go fishing, which made me a little uneasy. I mean, what kind of guy comes to Alaska and does not fish? Poets are just not normal.

Anyway, he was very busy. With luck I wouldn't see him again before he left town.

Then he came to the house. By this time, I was starting to go a little Edgar Allen Poe, hearing heartbeats under the floor, imagining stuffing Collins into a wall and hanging sheetrock over him. I almost convinced myself that he had come to Alaska just to expose and destroy me, an unknown short story writer and part-time adjunct writing instructor. Why would he do that? More grist for his lyrical mill. Poets are like that, I told myself: cruel and self-serving. Who knew how many stanzas he'd get out of the whole ugly affair at my expense. The bastard.

I tried to disarm him with friendliness. I plied him with fresh king salmon, halibut, local razor clams. I pushed numerous glasses of wine on him; he did not resist. He was relaxed, laughing, telling stories, the center of the party. Women were jockeying for positions near him on the couch. I kept pouring him wine. I thought I was in the clear.

Then Collins pulled me off to one side, wanting to talk privately. Sweat broke out on my arms and froze. Suddenly I could see how cleverly he had stalked me like a feeding carp. He'd made a perfect cast and set the bait—his friendship—right in front of me, and I'd swallowed it. Now he would strip-strike and set the hook. From his pocket he would pull a crumpled copy of my poem, torn out of the magazine, and say horrible, humiliating things about it, and about me. He'd phrase them so beautifully I'd wish I'd said them myself.

No. He shook my hand and thanked me for the party. He thanked my wife. He'd had a wonderful time. Okay, one more glass of wine, but then he really had to go. In a moment of clarity, I realized that he knew nothing of my poem. Now I wanted to hear him mention it. Driven by the need to be seen as a fellow poet, even a skulking, thieving, criminal of a poet, I slipped away to my office to get the magazine.

Years ago, in the first week of the first fiction-writing class I taught after finishing graduate school, a student turned in a plagiarized story. She was a mature, accomplished career woman who was taking the class for her own enjoyment, not a naive or confused young freshman. But the need to succeed in this class as she perceived it, and as I had certainly promoted it, drove her to shortcut the arduous process of creative writing. Instead of imagining characters and finding their stories, she borrowed characters from a nearly 100-year-old classic American story and stuck them in a new setting and gave them new names. The plot and its climax and the story's theme were unchanged, the relationships between the characters identical, some of the lines of description lifted nearly word for word from the original and altered just enough to update them.

I'd more or less forgotten the original story. It was one of many I'd read over the years in collections and anthologies as a student and teacher of fiction. When I looked at this student's manuscript I was haunted by the familiarity of it, but wanting to believe in her talent and wanting her to succeed nearly as much as she wanted to, I wrote that off to déjà vu.

When another, sharp-eyed student brought this borrowing to my attention, I confronted the author of the fraud. She hinted that maybe what she'd done was an homage, a tribute to the long-dead original author. But because she'd taken credit for the story first and only admitted the truth once she was caught, her argument was lost. There was a flap that went to the top of our department. The student left my class and was lucky she was not expelled from the college.

Now, facing my own guilt, I wondered about that student and about what we'd both done. True, her theft was no accident; she'd admitted as much. But how thinly can you slice ethics and literary originality? Must we take apart every sentence we write to see what we owe to our predecessors? And where does my embarrassing but convenient memory lapse really fall in the scheme of things?

I'm a fisherman, first and foremost. Small lies sort of come with the territory. I decided to give myself the benefit of the doubt. Call it relativism if you like, but in an age of false memoirs and clever bestselling novels that "re-imagine" characters from Melville and Austen, my sloppy use of a few lines of stolen imagery in a fishing poem seemed on a par with a corrupt defense contractor putting a phony quarter in a Pentagon parking meter—or so I convinced myself.

Still, I felt like I owed Billy Collins something. And I knew exactly what that was. I grabbed a copy of my story collection *Water of an Undetermined Depth*, generously signed it, and stuck it in Collins's hand as he prepared to leave. I took him by one elbow and turned him toward the front door. Before he realized what was happening he was walking down my driveway carrying my book. I figured he needed something to read on the long flight home from Alaska. With luck he wouldn't notice how much of it I stole from Tobias Wolff.

Chapter 10

The Killing Season

I've been having trouble killing things lately.

I noticed that about myself a couple months ago, back in the first week of March, when my friend Captain Ed Murphy asked me to go trolling for winter king salmon on his boat, the beautiful *Tulchina*, and I demurred. Most salmon fishing here in Southcentral Alaska doesn't start until summertime when the five species of Pacific salmon return to their natal rivers to spawn and cash in their genetic chips, and are within easy reach of a man with a rod and reel and a pair of waders. But a handful of boat owners, including Captain Ed, have discovered that nearby Kachemak Bay hosts seagoing adult salmon, feeding on the abundant local shrimp and baitfish schooling there year-round. And in the cold dark months when the rivers are frozen solid in their beds, the saltwater king fishery is a reason to live. God knows I can use all of those I can get.

No one in his right mind would turn down an offer to go fishing on stunningly beautiful Kachemak Bay at the time of year when the freezer is out of salmon fillets and winter's oppressive boredom is at its relentless worst. The Kenai Peninsula mountains and glaciers, and the rich bird life on the bay (puffins, kittiwakes, cormorants, and loons), are worth the boat ride alone. Even a dyed-in-the-wool fly fisher can appreciate the hopeful expectation vibrating in the tips of trolling rods when he's sitting in the lush comfort of the *Tulchina*'s warm cabin, sipping a coffee, watching the electronic screen festooned with little fish icons indicating previous salmon catches. Not to mention the hilarious companionship of Captain Ed. Still, when Ed called, I made some excuse about having a writing deadline or a class to teach and told him I could not go. Then I sat home in my office all day, wondering if he was catching anything, staring out at the late winter snow still covering the ground and trying to figure out why I had done that.

Now it's May, and the Anchor River behind my house officially opens for king salmon fishing in a week or so, and there is nothing I'd like better than to lay a quivering slab of fresh salmon on the grill when that happens. To do so I'll have to catch one, smash its head with a rock and slit its gills to bleed it out, and then bring it home and hack it into pieces like an unlucky secondary character in a Scorcese mob movie. All of which I have been doing to fish most of my life, but find a little disturbing lately.

That is an embarrassing thing for an Alaskan male to admit, maybe any male. I'm a manly guy. Ask anybody who knows me. I have a big moustache, a filthy mouth, a bad back, and a pickup truck full of more tools than a Home Depot. All the right stuff. Even so, I've been having trouble killing things lately.

Maybe it's just my age. Now that I'm retired and living with the knowledge that my own demise is not as far over the horizon as I once imagined, I'm less inclined to abbreviate the lives of other creatures—even tasty salmon. Maybe I just spend too much time alone here in my house in the woods thinking about stuff like this. Or maybe it is the fact that on March 6, 2004, a Saturday, my twenty-seven-year-old daughter, Lorien April Chiappone, died of cancer in a hospital in Buffalo, New York, and that ever since then I have had a hard time watching living things expire.

That could be a coincidence. But I doubt it.

As is true for many fishermen of a certain age, I started purposefully killing fish as a small boy: sunfish, bullheads, yellow perch, rock bass. Some of my happiest memories include white rope stringers of panfish dangling from the handlebars of an old blue Schwinn. When I was a teenager, I started hunting too, and I loved to bring game home and watch my mother cook it: grouse, rabbits, big gray squirrels. I remember a pheasant that ended up in Sunday spaghetti sauce. How improbable is that? A Southeast Asian bird, shot in New York State, made into Italian food.

Those are good memories, although I have to admit I never cared for the gritty, hands-on realities of hunting: a rabbit's steaming innards pouring out onto the frozen weeds, the sickening crunch of a bird's neck breaking in my hands. I liked the *idea* of the sport, but when it came to the blood and guts, I was a complete cupcake. I gave up hunting altogether sometime in my mid-twenties, claiming I was too busy trying to support my growing family. I kept fishing though. Fish were easier to kill somehow.

The fact is, something has to die for me to live. To live authentically, I need to kill that thing myself. I really don't want to do that anymore.

I suppose I could give up meat altogether and trade being persistently neurotic for the glow of sanctimony that seems to come from eating three uninteresting, unsatisfying, and unpleasantly gray-green meals each day. Or I could really confuse myself and only eat chickens and fish, but not sheep or cows or pigs for reasons too logically abstruse to explain—even to myself. No thanks. I'll stick with the hypocrisy I'm familiar with: I'll continue to cook my signature baked veal shanks and wash them down with a fine cardboard box cabernet and simply not ask how the little cow is getting along without ankles.

Then there's catch-and-release fishing, which—meat hunting for salmon aside—I have been practicing for many years, and I intend to keep on doing so: trout and steelhead mostly, but also bonefish and other prized saltwater fish too precious to kill. Like vegetarianism, there are generally two arguments for the catch-and-release ethic: one logical and one moral. (Vegetarians may start out talking about nutrition, but it isn't long before that halo begins to glow overhead.) And, predictably, the latter is much, much harder to argue than the former.

Realistically, if we all took home a stringer full of trout the way anglers did when I was young, we would empty all the rivers in the country in a short time. So, out of necessity, we pragmatically release fish in order to keep their species from going extinct. We do this so that we can catch them and release them again and again. It's absurd, but it does keep the fish populations healthy—if not happy. And therein lies the moral rub.

Let's face it: sticking a hook into a fish, pulling it—gasping—out of its element to take a photo of it, and then letting it go again simply for the purpose of making the creature available for repeated abuse of this same kind is hard to dress up as enlightened. It's entirely irrational, not to mention cruel and barbaric. The only question remaining is, *So what*? Sure, outsmarting a creature with a brain the size of a pea may not seem like the kind of accomplishment that requires photo evidence to commemorate it. But when done in a sporting fashion it is a challenging, satisfying, and more or less harmless way for a person to stay interested in getting through the years he has left on this earth. If ruining the day for a creature with no apparent complex feelings and very little cerebral cortex is the worst sin I commit in this lifetime, send me to hell for it, brother. I'll do the time happily.

But all this talk about life and death and people getting what they deserve reminds me that I'm avoiding the real subject here.

Grief is a subject worth avoiding. But I'm learning it's difficult to predict when it will rear its unruly head, or in what form it will appear when it does. A couple months after my daughter died, I was working on my house with a young friend, Doug. The fishing season had not started yet, so we were working on the back deck, hammering away in the warm spring air. I had been in a fog since Lori's death, but the pain was numbing out a little by then and it's possible that I even stopped thinking about her altogether for a few hours that day, busy with the work at hand, enjoying the good weather, the company of a friend.

One of our cats was out: Ed, a dark brown Siamese the size of a prehistoric beaver. We usually keep our cats indoors because of their murderous habit of killing voles and shrews and lining them up on the doorstep. I can't stand to see even rodents die anymore. But Ed the cat is so old and fat and slow, you take one look at him and just know that the only thing he'll ever kill again is a can of mackerel.

Still, somehow that day Ed managed to murder a beautiful short-tailed weasel, about nine inches long, and not quite dead when I found it lying on its side on the bottom step of the porch where Ed had proudly set it. The weasel looked unscathed but for a clump of mashed fur, damp with cat spittle, on the back of its broken neck. Windpipe crushed, it clawed the air with its front feet and gasped for a few last breaths. I stood there gaping, unable to look away from it. Doug, intuiting that I was in only slightly better shape than the poor weasel, told me that he thought it would survive if he hid it in the wood pile, safe from the magpies and ravens until it could snap out of it and run again. It's good to have friends who will lie to you when you need them to. You can't count on always being able to do that for yourself.

In late February of 2004, I spent several days with my daughter at my brother's house back east on the shore of Lake Ontario, near the famous trophy brown trout streams of that region. My brother and his wife were in Florida at the time. Lori was very ill with the disease, and ravished by the brutal treatments we visit upon cancer victims in our unwillingness to let death win too easily. But she was in good spirits in spite of all that. We had the house to ourselves, and late in the evenings we watched DVDs. She was in pain from the uterine tumors, and she sat in my brother's lounge chair with a bag of ice pressed against her lap and a heating pad on her lower back, pointing out flaws in the continuity of the film *Gladiator*. "How could Ridley Scott not see that?" she snorted. She was a merciless critic, just like her old man. Sometimes, momentarily, I forgot exactly why we were together there like that. I hope she did too.

One day we went to the Roswell Park Cancer Institute in Buffalo, where she was about to start taking an experimental chemo cocktail in a pharmaceutical trial. To keep the trial results legit, Lori needed to be "randomized," a transitive verb I had never heard before. There could be no inadvertent bias in the pairing of the patient and the particular combination of deadly poisons they were experimenting with. Randomized. To me, everything about this seemed plenty random. Why her, for example? I had lived in the same industrial upstate environment for thirty years (longer than she had) before moving to Alaska. Even worse, I had worked in the chemical plants. I had smoked Kools and played in a band in smoke-filled bars for ten years. Why her and not me? Why not some other unlucky person we didn't even know? That hospital was full of those. Okay, that was a very ungenerous thought. But if you ever have to go through this, be prepared to entertain a few.

Another day we went to the Seneca Indian Casino in the city of Niagara Falls. We played video poker. We ate crab legs. I didn't even know Lori liked crab legs. That would become my explanation for why I seemed to be handling the grief so well. "I hardly knew her," I'd say when asked how I was dealing with her death. "I'm fine," I'd say. "Fine."

You'll have to forgive me if I can't get overly concerned with a trout's problems. Even the ones that I cause. I'm sorry.

Shortly after the weasel incident, I started carrying spiders out of the house whenever I found them struggling up the smooth porcelain sides of the bathroom sink. At one time I would have simply run the water and let them take their chances with the drainpipes. Not anymore. I cupped them in the bathroom glass and slid them out onto the back porch. Nothing was going to die under my nose any longer—not even arachnids. The cats were not allowed out at all. Frustrated, they turned their hunting skills on torpid windowsill houseflies, eating them with a nauseating crunch of carapace I could hear across the room. I would yell, "Wait! Wait! Stop!" But, in answer, there would only be another crunch.

I could not save everything, but at least I was not involved directly in anything's destruction. I don't think I killed any salmon that summer for the first time in over two decades in Alaska. I don't remember digging clams either. It looked like I was going to have to join the enormous ranks of those in denial and let other people do my dirty work for me. I don't think that's healthy, but I was not killing anything with my own hands for a while.

I had to stay busy. I decided to put in a small rubber pond next to the garage. My wife, Lin, and I went to the local feed and pet supply store, The Wagon Wheel, on Homer Spit Road. There we bought five tiny goldfish for the pond. The kid at the store referred to them as "feeders." But these five lucky ones were never going to be fed to anything. Not by me. Watching them swimming in the rubber pond, I remembered reading, many years ago when I was a kid, a *Field and Stream* article about using live goldfish as bait for largemouth bass. I thought about ramming hooks through the backs of our little feeders and cringed. This was not a good train of thought for a fisherman to be boarding. I thought about something else.

The goldfish lived in the rubber pond all summer, and in the fall we moved them to a thirty-gallon aquarium in our living room near the woodstove. We've had them for years now. They are probably five inches long and have names: Eenie, Meenie, Miney, Moby, and Sylvia. They will live forever, and when Lin and I die peacefully and at great age, the goldfish and the cats will fight over our estate.

I was doing fine, see? Sense of humor intact. Fine.

Then this happened: We bought a plecostomus, a suction-mouthed algae eater, to clean the green slime off the aquarium glass. I came downstairs one morning to find it floating on the surface, too close to death for my tastes. I poked it with the little wire-rimmed net and it swam to the bottom and then lethargically drifted back up. My heart started hammering. I called for Lin. She came, almost at a run, the sound of panic in my voice startling her. I was staring down into the tank. I said something that made no sense. She took the net away from me and assured me the fish was just resting. It died later that day and we replaced it with a second plecostomus the following week. That one lasted a month. No more plecostomus. I'm not that fine.

I'VE KILLED A LOT OF fish on purpose, of course: hundreds of salmon in my years in Alaska, for example, even with the most inefficient method of all—a fly rod. I murder enough Kenai River sockeye each summer to last all winter, canned in pint jars. I've killed and cooked or smoked silvers by the dozens over the years, and I generally catch at least one Anchor River king each season, and one or more out there in the salt on Captain Ed's boat. Like most coastal Alaskans, I've killed some halibut too. But for sheer numbers, nothing can match the body count on the razor clams I've sent to invertebrate heaven.

Four years after Lori's death, I went clamming with my friend Pete. Around our house, Pete is fondly known as Commodore Clam. I think the man can spot a razor clam dimple from the top of the bluff overlooking Cook Inlet. He may be able to see clams on the other side of the inlet, forty miles away. Thanks to his guidance, I was home cleaning a nice bucket of clams when I had an episode much worse than the weasel or plecostomus moments.

Bear in mind that I had already killed over a hundred clams that summer. They are brainless, spineless, faceless bivalves. It's almost like digging fishy-smelling potatoes. Clearly, my willingness to slaughter them meant I was getting better, mentally healthier. It had been four years. The grief over Lori's death was beginning to fade into the past, right? I had gone dipnetting for red salmon earlier that summer; it was a joyous and bloody massacre. I had murdered a couple nice halibut, impaling them with the gaff and then happily beating their brains out all over the deck of the *Tulchina*. I was a high-functioning, meat-eating man once more.

Almost.

Lin was at work and I was cleaning the clams, alone in the kitchen. Pete had shown me a way to speed up the process by blanching the live clams in boiling water to kill them instantly and open their shells. I had a large pasta pot boiling on the stove. I would throw four or five live clams into the water and then lift the basket out and run them under the cold tap to stop them from cooking. The meat separated from the shells cleanly, and the guts could be cut out with a quick slice of the knife. As a large glass bowl filled with the tasty clam meat, the plastic bucket of live ones steadily emptied. Almost finished, I laid the last four living clams on the kitchen counter and waited for the water in the pot to come to a boil once more.

All razor clams are more or less identical. Their "noses," the long snout-like feeding tubes that reach to the surface of the sand, and their "feet," the diggers they use to burrow into the sea bottom, are the same rubbery, tan-colored flesh on every one of them. But there on my kitchen counter, right before my eyes, was a strange pink-and-brown-striped clam like I'd never seen before. And although the other three remaining regular-looking clams were slammed tight inside their shells and lying quietly on the countertop waiting to be boiled alive, this weird pink one was madly digging at the Formica with its foot, twisting and heaving and futilely attempting to burrow into the plastic.

For a second I thought I was hallucinating. Then I thought it was a practical joke. I actually thought my friend Pete had slipped some sort of gag gift, wind-up clam into my bucket (I wouldn't put it past him). But this was a real live clam. Too alive. And it did not plan on getting itself boiled, gutted, chopped to pieces, sautéed with garlic, and dumped over linguini. OK, maybe a clam can't think that far ahead, but the son-of-bitch wanted to live! That much was indisputable.

I had a panic attack. I went dizzy. My heart felt like it was swelling and shrinking over and over. (Yes, I realize that is more or less how a heart works. But you aren't supposed to be acutely aware of it.) I watched the creature struggling, levering its shell off the countertop, straining and writhing like an overturned turtle as it tried to burrow into the Formica. I kept staring at it, waiting for it to stop and lie still like the others. But it would not. The anxiety roared through me.

The striped clam looked different from the others. That was the worst part. It looked different. It acted differently. It was an individual. And it wanted to live! I started hyperventilating. The water was boiling. The strainer basket danced in the pot, rattling impatiently. I kept thinking, *I am not going to make it if I kill this clam.* My head was coming unscrewed. I really thought I was going crazy. I *was* going crazy.

We live in the woods, out of sight of our few neighbors. There was no one to talk to, no one to show this clam. If I phoned Lin at work, she would hear the hysteria in my voice. She has lived with me for nearly thirty years. She knows how these things go. I'm not the sanest patient in the asylum on my best days. She'd be frantic. I didn't call.

Instead, I did what I had to do.

Hours later, when Lin got home, we had drinks and ate the clam appetizers I had pounded and dipped in egg and parmesan cheese and breaded, and fried in olive oil. I must have been uncommonly quiet. She studied me and asked what was going on. I hesitated. I tried to blow it off—just another one of my moods. Of course, I can't keep anything from the woman. I finally told her the whole story about the strange clam, the way it was digging into the countertop so desperately. My wife is used to my antics. It is my sworn obligation to make her laugh at least once every day, and no joke is too ridiculous, too childish or too stupid for me to attempt. But Lin is a trained counselor. She could see that I was not joking.

She said, "You took that clam back to the beach and let it go, didn't you?"

I had indeed. In what was perhaps the first incident of catch and release in the history of clam digging, I did just that. When that strange clam wouldn't stop struggling, I finally turned off the stove, put the unique creature back in the few inches of seawater remaining in the five gallon plastic bucket and carried it out to the truck. I was at the beach in six minutes. The tide was coming in by then. I put the truck in four-wheel and drove to the edge of the water, not wanting any of the men at the boat launch to see me carry a clam to the ocean and gently set it in the muddy surf line. I drove back home, restarted the stove and finished cleaning the remaining three normal clams. I got out the meat hammer and the breadcrumbs and made them into cocktail snacks.

I had to kill those last three or I was really going to have a problem. Even I could see that.

I'm just a fisherman, but I think it is fair to opine that one component of our humanity is the ability (and the luxury) to choose which organisms around us we are willing to kill and which we are not. This is the philosophical side of catch-and-release fishing that arguably takes the idea beyond mere fishery resource management. By choosing to let a fish go, we have a sense of being in control of another creature's life, and by extension, control of our own life. If, out of necessity, we had to grab and stuff into our mouths every edible thing in our paths, just to stay alive—every insect, grub, worm, spider, lizard or fish that hopped or crawled or swam into our line of sight, every trout we caught—we would not feel in control, or even very human. Conversely, not being able to stop a death when we want to, say our own child's, for example, is a dispiriting reminder that this sense of control, this notion that we get to choose what lives or dies is situational at best.

In the spring of 2003, I was driving between Anchorage and our home at Anchor Point when my cell phone went off and I saw an unusual area code displayed. I answered to find my daughter Lori on the line. Lori had been about three when her mother and I divorced. She and I had been friendly over the quarter century we lived on opposite sides of the continent, but we were not close. It was extremely odd for her to call out of the blue this way. I pulled over into the gravel parking lot of a building supply place in the town of Soldotna, near the world-famous Kenai River, which was running high and ice choked and still unfishable at that time of year. I asked her what was going on, and she said, "It seems I have a little cancer."

She was fit and strong and otherwise healthy: a cheerful, tattooed and pierced, twenty-seven-year-old, neo-hippie Deadhead with an education in outdoor recreational studies and a yen for camping and canoes and such. She was supposed to be married in the fall of the year she died. Her fiancé, Alex, is a chemical engineer with a good job. They had put money down on a house. They had a dog.

This is the killing season. Captain Ed is already out there trolling for king salmon in the bay. The freshwater opener is May 15 on the Anchor River. There is a monster low tide coming up on the Memorial Day weekend and the clamming should be great. Anglers are getting halibut offshore at Anchor Point a few minutes away from my house. It's time.

Only two jars of Lin's home-canned salmon remain on the shelf in our pantry. There are no more bags of clam meat left in the freezer. I have to kill something, soon. If I can. If I'm healthy enough. I have to. It is what a lifelong fisherman does.

At the time of Lori's initial diagnosis, the doctors at the Roswell Park Cancer Institute in Buffalo—given the relatively nonaggressive type of tumor they thought they were dealing with—declared that my daughter had a 90 percent probability of becoming completely well again. They would catch that cancer early, they said. And Lori would be treated and released in no time at all.

Completely well again.

I like the sound of that.

I wonder what my odds are.

Chapter 11

Requiem for a River Bend

GONE

Last fall, I lost a quarter mile of the river that flows behind my house here at Anchor Point, Alaska. After nearly three decades fishing the big bend that used to lie within sight of my living room, I have to say it was a little disconcerting to find it had become a high and dry oxbow remnant overnight, when the rain-swollen river blasted a new channel and took its water there. My river bend is gone.

The Anchor River, thirty feet wide and shallow enough to wade across in most places, starts in the soggy tundra of the Caribou Hills of the southern Kenai Peninsula, and runs westward for twenty miles before passing my house here on a heavily wooded promontory overlooking the little river valley. Three miles farther downstream, the river crosses the beach at Anchor Point and enters the saltwater of Cook Inlet.

The erstwhile bend was a big J hook that slowed the current and created holding water for anadromous fish, which in turn created some of the best road-accessible fly fishing for wild steelhead anywhere in the United States. But the new channel flows in a featureless line from the top of the J to the point of the hook, basically a quarter mile chute as straight as a drag strip, and as fishless.

It's not like this can be undone. Recently I read a commentary on memoir writing in which the author said that memoirists act on a longing to revisit parts of their pasts in the way that rivers seek to return to their old, former channels, now dry and overgrown with brush and trees. It's a lovely metaphor. But anyone who lives on a river, or anyone who ever took earth science in high school, knows that just the opposite is true: as a river ages, it leaves those doomed oxbows behind forever. Driven only by gravity, a river's singular intent (if I may continue with what Ruskin called *the pathetic fallacy* of personification and intentionality here) is to carve the shortest path from its source to the sea.

Yes, the Anchor has constantly changed over the two and a half decades I've fished it. That's what rivers do. Season after season, fishable pockets of water have come and gone like fashion trends. But it was incremental. With each small shift in holding water, I had to make adjustments in my fishing which added variety and new challenges. But that bend was a huge geological feature, a major curve in the spine of that river that contained three great steelhead holes. Small changes notwithstanding, I had foolishly assumed those holes would endure—at least as long as I did.

It's a ten-minute walk from my house to the dry oxbow that was once the bend, and only a few steps more to the new channel nearby where the river relocated itself. When I last saw it, just before ice-up, the new stretch of river was still churning through a maze of downed spruce and cottonwood trees it had bowled over on its shortcut to the sea—their yellow leaves fluttering madly in the current, roots reaching for the sky. It's true that, over time, as the ice and spring floods gouge declivities and undercut banks and wash away the fallen timber, new pockets and holding water will form in that channel. Even so, making new friends does not entirely ameliorate the loss of old ones.

OF FISH AND FRIENDS

The Anchor River is home to three species of salmon (kings, silvers and pinks), steelhead trout, and Dolly Varden char. By the time the stretch of river behind my house opens to fishing on August 1st, the kings are dead and gone, and it's a little too early for silvers or steelhead. But, at the top of the J where the bend once began, a wide slow run we called the Meadow Hole was invariably full of small Dollies.

Dolly Varden—pink-and-purple-spotted creatures, supposedly named after a Dickens character who wore similarly colorful hats—are a lot like brook trout. Only even less wary. When they're feeding on swimming caddis nymphs they'll hit just about anything you drag through the surface film on a tight line, which makes Dollies great fish for newcomers to the sport. And, between the Dollies' predictability (steelhead and salmon can be as uncooperative as an ex-spouse) and the wide-open and brush-free banks of the Meadow Hole (hence the name), it was a wonderful place to introduce novices to fly fishing.

The youngest angler I ever took there was then six-year-old Ross Bass, son of my longtime business partner. Ross showed up wielding a pushbutton spinning rig he was already adept with. So, I tied a nymph on the end of his line a couple feet below his Goofy bobber (a floating plastic Disney character the size of a navel orange) and he was soon into squirming, foot-long Dollies. Because Ross was a little too young to appreciate the sublime pointlessness of catch and release, we built a corral of rocks in the shallows and filled it with the fish he landed. I told him we'd take the whole batch home to show his mother at the end of the day. When the Dollies found their way out of the pen—as I was almost certain they would—Ross was only moderately disappointed. He'd done what he'd come to do: catch fish. Purposely deceiving a small child aside, I felt that it was a good day at the Meadow Hole.

At the other end of the age range, another memorable first-timer was a woman in her early seventies named Cecilia. A late-in-life transplant to Alaska from New York City, Cecilia was great looking, and an adventurous spirit in her knee-high rubber boots and perfectly coiffed hair. She was talkative and good company, and we gabbed cheerfully on the walk to the water, down the steep promontory trail, and through a jumble of beetle-killed spruce trees stacked like pick-up sticks for giants. Given her age, I worried a bit about the walk home, a lung-straining climb back up the same trail, zigzagging around, over, and under the dead trees. Though a dozen years younger than she, I'll admit that, in recent years, upon reaching the top of the hill I've begun pausing to sit on a stump before staggering the last hundred yards to the house. But Cecilia, buoyed by an afternoon of sunshine and fast Dolly action, and probably by the dizzying misconception that fishing would always be like that, marched uphill through the obstacle course and straight to the back porch, chatting all the way. I wheezed out an answer or two, when required.

I've taken several other neophytes down that path to the river over the years. But the bend was not just for beginners. Later each autumn, the Dollies would abandon it and move upriver to feed on salmon eggs behind silvers spawning in the headwaters. And then the steelhead would slip into my backyard. October is winter in Alaska, and that means time to stow away cartoon bobbers and say goodbye to attractive older women, time to climb into winter undies and heavy waders, to clamp lead on leaders and make short, thudding casts for often fruitless hours. Not the kind of fishing that would endear the sport to most novitiates. It's time to fish for steelhead.

THE BEND HOLE

A good hole for winter steelheading used to lie just downstream from the Meadow Hole in the crook of the elbow on the J. There the water cut a trench against the far bank, good holding water for steelhead.

As with most steelhead water, the Bend Hole offered some productive seasons, and some poor. But when it ran hot, it could be a scorcher. One day, walking downstream from the Meadow Hole, I found a pair of twenty-something anglers occupying the deep cut at the bend. Screened by a wall of willows, the pair didn't notice I was within earshot. As one knelt to release a steelhead, his partner asked, "How many is that now?" And the first guy answered, "Twelve."

That's how good the Bend Hole could be.

THE FLAMING

Farther downstream, at tip of the J, where the final good hole on my river bend used to be, there is now a wide, still lagoon. This is spill-over water from the new channel blasting past the oxbow and backing up into the low end of it. On the cool September afternoon that I discovered the big changes, dozens of fingerlings—salmon and steelhead parr, or young Dollies perhaps—were gulping midges and late season mayflies off the surface of the frog water. But it used to be a hell of a steelhead hole. Originally referred to as the Lower Bend Hole, about fifteen years ago it was renamed by one of my oldest fishing pals, Gomer.

I met Gomer in the late 1980s when he still lived in Anchorage and worked for one of the oil companies. Over the years, we fished together from Kodiak Island to some of the greatest trout streams of Bristol Bay. I've never met anyone more fun to share an inflatable raft, a gravel bar, or a campfire with.

Gomer had what might be called a personality of excess. In those days, he ate too much, drank too much, and smoked too much (he was quitting cigarettes every day for all the years I fished with him). He laughed loudly and frequently in a high giggle, like a coyote with hiccups, and kept a line of entertaining (and mostly apocryphal) stories going for hours. The guy fished like he thought he was going to have to give it up at any moment. In the subarctic, where the summer sun can own the sky for eighteen or twenty hours, keeping up with him was an extreme sport in itself.

One October, on the Columbus Day weekend, Gomer and our mutual friend Henry, an airline pilot with similar habits, made the two-hundred-mile drive from Anchorage to Anchor Point to fish behind my house. The steelhead run peaks on the Anchor River around the second week of October, and the water can get crowded. All weekend, Gomer, Henry, and I found ourselves shut out of our favorite holes by strangers who had made the two-mile trek to the Bend Hole from the bridge, the nearest public access point.

To celebrate the Italian explorer's holiday, the Anchorage hedonists brought a box of gourmet comestibles from one of the tonier grocery stores in Alaska's big city. So, late one afternoon, tired of being crowded out of the most productive water anyway, I headed back up to the house to start braising some veal shanks. Not surprisingly, Gomer and Henry stayed on the river and fished until dark. When they finally arrived at the back porch—Gomer gasping for breath between puffs on his cigarette—they ranted about the appalling lack of streamside etiquette they'd suffered when they finally got a shot at the Lower Bend Hole.

As stories of riparian abominations tend to, this one involved a gang of rude non-flyfishers. Gomer and Henry had no sooner parked themselves in the productive hole, when two (or was it four?) philistines with spinning rods, waded in upstream and down and proceeded to cast hardware across their lines (also a familiar trope in these tales). Of course, it wouldn't be a story unless the bastards started hauling in steelhead—which, no surprise, they did.

Suffice it to say that the Lower Bend was forever after referred to as the Flaming Ass Hole.

CHANGE

Nothing stays the same for long. The older you get, the more you quit trying to believe otherwise. Not that it makes it much easier.

Last fall, with the bend holes gone, I brooded and fished a long deep run called Dolly Land, a bit downstream from my house. Dolly Land got its name because the little char were so numerous there they could be positively pestiferous if you were trying for steelhead. Even so, it was also one of the most consistently productive steelhead runs on the river. Or it used to be, until last September. Without the big bend upstream from it, the current now races into Dolly Land filling the best parts of the run with rubble carved out of the new channel. More good water gone.

Not all the changes in the river have been geological. Like almost everything else in the world, the Internet has had an effect on it too. If you google "Alaskan steelhead fishing," your trusty computer will point you to the Kenai Peninsula and the three rivers there that have steelhead runs—including the one in my backyard. As I said, there are very few places left to fish for wild steelhead on the road system in America and fewer yet in most other countries. These days, the Anchor can get more than a little busy wherever it rubs up against the road. In response to the ever-increasing pressure, the Alaska Department of Fish and Game recently shortened the season even further.

More fishermen, fewer days to fish, less good water. Things change.

I grew up in an industrial area of the Great Lakes, nearly devoid of gamefish in the '60s and '70s when I lived there. Maybe that's why I spent more than twenty years building a house on a wild salmon and trout stream in Alaska. And now that the work is complete, and

I'm retired and have more time to fish, a geological phenomenon has eradicated the best holes within walking distance of the house, and the season is so short a couple good rainstorms can effectively eliminate it. It sounds like the comic restaurant review: "The food was terrible, and the portions were too small." It's a good thing I'm a fan of irony.

MORE CHANGE

Today, Ross is in sixth grade and so busy with school activities he'll have long outgrown that Goofy bobber by the time he gets back down here; Cecilia, after several harsh Alaskan winters, has moved back to Manhattan; Henry has retired to New Hampshire, and lives on a lake with a long Native American name and smallmouth bass; and Gomer now lives in Tennessee and hasn't fished since a tumor on his spine put him in a wheelchair a couple years ago. When I talked to him on the phone this week, he said he was starting radiation treatments on what little of his pancreas the surgeons deemed prudent to leave behind in his most recent operation. But he didn't want to talk about that. Mostly he wanted to know how the river fished last fall.

I didn't have much good to report. The truth is, I stopped fishing in mid-October, after only a couple trips down to the river. I told myself it was because of the loss of the bend. But maybe one of the things that kept me from making the hike was the sudden awareness that the river valley bottomland is filled with the impressions of much older oxbows. The dead river channels closest to the foot of the promontory are the oldest and most filled-in. They probably ran heavy with glacial melt water as the last glaciers deposited the big gravel esker my house is built upon. Now they faintly reveal themselves as crescent-moon curves of willow or twisted black spruce jutting up from the wet grasses. Closer to the river, the trail crosses several much more recently deceased channels. They are now deep trenches, at least one with a trickle of remnant river current still detectable in the tannic water like a weak pulse. Others have become long narrow ponds, stagnant and leafed-clogged, their muddy bottoms gouged by moose hooves.

In a few places I recognize the ghosts of runs that have vanished in my own lifetime, holes I remember fishing not that many years ago. There is one we called the Eagle's Nest Hole. I believe it was Gomer who blundered upon it and the great fishing it offered. The namesake eagle's nest, now abandoned and crumbling, is still visible high in the big cottonwood that towered over the hidden hole. My fishing journal shows that I caught steelhead directly under that nest every day for thirteen days in a row one October in the 1990s. Today, a hundred feet of gravel and dry river rocks lie between that tree and the closest water.

On the other hand, maybe I chose to stay at home and watch the river from the chair closest to the woodstove so many days last season because the fused vertebrae in my neck and lower back, and their attendant titanium rods and screws, were making the march through the fallen spruce and across the boot-sucking wetlands more trouble than the fishing—such as it was—could make up for.

Yet now, deep in the dark heart of another Alaskan winter with months to go before the new season opener, I can't remember the geezer aches and pains as clearly as those sunny days fishing with friends, Dollies flashing in the Meadow Hole like little bolts of underwater lightning, big red-cheeked steelhead bulling into the tailout of the Lower Bend.

Two things I know for sure.

Rivers straighten with age, while men bend.

And, secondly, come August, those fish will be out there somewhere, and so will I.

For Bill Lelake, 1945–2013

Chapter 12

The Winter Face

It was nearly the end of March and still snowing. Although technically spring now that the vernal equinox was upon us, the morning sky was as dull and gray as a tax auditor, and the falling flakes had the same sickly pallor as the aging snow already blanketing the woods. Somewhere out there under a winter's worth of white stuff was a box of steelhead flies that fell from my vest on the way down the hill to the river last fall. I wouldn't be needing them anytime soon; the river was a frozen white stripe winding through the wetlands below, and it would stay that way for weeks to come.

There's a reason no one ever talks about "the dead of summer" or "the summer of our discontent." There's a reason Stravinsky's *The Rite of Spring* sounds like the work of a madman and that March is a good month to murder a Caesar. Say what you will about the sun and the angle of the earth's axis at this time of year. I know winter when I see it.

I was not, I repeat, *not* suffering from seasonal affective disorder (SAD), a depressive condition common in the dark months at northern latitudes around the globe. SAD is caused in part by lack of sunlight and subsequent low levels of serotonin in the brain. On March 21, even here in Southcentral Alaska, I was receiving the same twelve hours of daylight bathing everyone else on the planet. Theoretically I should have been as cheerful as the well-tanned souls who woke up on the equator that morning, serotonin positively coursing through me. Theoretically.

No, this wasn't about light. This was about snow, and this was about ice. Truth be known, this was about not having cast a fly in nearly five months and knowing that fishing season was still two months off. This was about NFS, Not Fishing Syndrome—an underdiagnosed malaise whose sufferers weep when the first fly-fishing magazines arrive in January, and lie awake at night thinking unkind thoughts about the authors of articles titled, "Spring Fishing Tactics for Early Season Trout!" Early season here is June.

My wife finds it astonishing that I persist in responding so poorly to our long winters. She argues that a person who has lived in Alaska and seen the river turn to ice each October for twenty-four years in a row, a person who has shoveled snow in twenty-four consecutive Aprils and even a few Mays, shouldn't be surprised that the first day of our putative spring always resembles a scene from a PBS special about Antarctica.

But my wife was off to work, and I stood on the porch wearing light cotton pajamas to honor the official change of seasons and hammered the big round thermometer with my coffee cup to see if the arrow had jammed. The thermometer was sticking with its story: 19 degrees. I looked up into the gloom as those famously individual and unique snowflakes fluttered down, realizing that I despised each one in an individual and unique way.

Back inside at my desk, wet slippers drying on the radiator, I tried tying flies—which isn't fishing but is related to fishing and can be done wearing pajamas, even in winter. I could only stay interested in bonefish and tarpon patterns. Just looking at them conjured images of mangrove islands, sandy flats sparkling in the Caribbean sun. I could almost feel the heat, smell the steaming lagoons, hear the cries of egrets and night herons. Then one of our local eagles soared past at eye level in the ravine next to our house, yanking me from my reverie. I watched it disappear into a curtain of fog and snow hanging over the river valley. When I turned back to the vise, I caught my reflection in the magnifying lens on my tying lamp. Staring back at me was a white-stubbled wretch with hospital hair and a look of bewildered defeat. He looked like someone who hadn't fished in five months. It was my winter face.

Five months. That's how long the river had been frozen. That's how long every drop of fresh water within fifty miles had been frozen. That's how long fishing had meant drilling a hole through two-foot-thick ice. I realize some folks truly enjoy that. But after a lifetime spent learning to cast a fly, lowering a line straight down to the fish sounds a little like shooting clay pigeons in a box on the floor. In fact, casting, the aspect of fly fishing that most distinguishes it from other types of angling and the thing that makes it so special, is what I miss the most in winter. The pleasure of getting the line in the air and putting the fly where you want it almost makes up for the knowledge that real salmon eggs, flashing spinners, or deep-running plugs often catch more fish than our fur-and-feather creations do. So I decided that, winter or no winter, if I couldn't fish at least I could go outside and practice casting.

Even if medical experts have failed to make the obvious connection between lack of fishing and winter blues, their advice to fight depression by getting outdoors and exercising is sound. It's either that or keep moving cocktail hour a little earlier each day, until one morning in February you find yourself dunking your Pop-Tart in a vodka tonic while staring at a television where a Pennsylvania groundhog studies its shadow.

But the real reason I needed to practice was that in a couple weeks I was going fishing in Mexico, where long, accurate casts are often required. I can't actually make long, accurate casts and probably never will—certainly not with two weeks of repetitively entrenching my bad casting habits further into my muscle memory. But the thought that my sloppy casting might make our Mexican bonefish guide mutter things about me in Spanish (or worse, in English) was enough to convince me to venture out into the winter wasteland, rod in hand. I wanted to time it to coincide with my wife's return from work. Then it would appear that I'd been doing something besides moping around the house all day, something healthy and outdoorsy. So around four o'clock I got dressed, climbed into my boots, picked up my 8-weight rod, and went outside.

We built our house in a dense spruce forest, and it remains a dense spruce forest to this day because my wife is on a first-name basis with every tree. I might as well suggest microwaving one of the cats as crank up the chainsaw in her presence. Consequently, we have no yard, just snow-laden conifers closely encircling the house. The only patch of open ground is behind the shop, where the spruce trees fade to willows and muskeg sloping downhill toward the river.

With snow falling since Halloween, I was post-holing up to my zipper as I waded into the drifts to practice casting. That sounds like sheer idiocy, but even so, just carrying a rod in the general direction of the river *felt* like going fishing—and it beat pacing around the house wondering how long it was until cocktail hour.

Behind the shop, I laid a three-foot length of two-by-four on the snow at the edge of the forest, stepped back, and squinted until it became a bonefish. Of course in real life I will never see a three-foot bonefish. And if I do I'll have a heart attack and collapse into the sea before I manage to get off a cast. But when you are casting to lumber, you really want an encouragingly large target.

Fifty feet off from the boardfish, I stripped out line and decided what direction the two-by-four was swimming and which end was its head. The first few casts fell short, the line catching on the crusted snow. I threw harder. The fly—a huge pink tarpon fly with the hook clipped off—lofted on the breeze and landed a dozen feet behind the boardfish. Double-hauling ferociously, I finally got some distance, only to drop the line right across the boardfish's back. I could already hear the guide sucking tropical air over his teeth.

So it went. Sometimes I actually made a good cast, laying the hookless hot-pink fly on the snow a few feet in front of the two-by-four and imagining myself replicating that cast on my first real live Mexican bonefish. I ignored the casts that went nowhere because I was standing on the line, and the ones that slapped the back of the boardfish or landed way behind it, and the ones that sailed into the spruce trees beyond. No, when I got to Mexico, all my casts would be like the one that landed where it was supposed to. Practice makes perfect.

The trouble with practice-casting is that it's no more interesting than any other form of necessary exercise. Without an actual live fish to cast to, I lost interest in about nine minutes. It was snowing again, my legs were wet, and my fingers too numb to control the line, itself so cold it coiled like wire. I considered cutting silhouettes of more realistic fish from plywood—bonefish, tarpon, snook, some tailing permit, maybe a mutton snapper or two. I'd set them all over the snow and stand in the middle, rotating like a dervish casting at will. But even in my fish-deprived state, I knew it would take more than a school of wooden fish to offset the boredom of casting to stationary targets. I almost reeled in my frozen fly line and called it a day, and then my wife came home from work and accidentally let the cats out.

WE HAVE FOUR SIAMESE FELINES I call The Reservoir Cats. Three are eighteen-pounders, real Boone and Crockett specimens. The fourth one, "the baby," is a grumpy little guy about half the others' size. As my wife loves cats even more than trees, she has spoiled and enormously overfed them. Well, maybe I've had a little to do with that myself.

Ed is the oldest and heaviest, a "seal-point" Siamese well on his way to becoming the size and shape of an actual seal. Here is a poem I wrote for him.

House Cat in Retirement

Now you are so fat that
birds walk away from you,
mice laugh until little mouse tears
roll down their tiny whiskered faces.
Even yarn is no longer afraid.

Last summer Ed was attacked by something with very sharp teeth, but he's so fat that the predator couldn't grip anything except one of Ed's near vestigial legs. Thanks to modern veterinary science (and modern credit cards), Ed's leg is whole again, but so is our awareness of what's out there. Last steelhead season, a coyote walked out onto the gravel bar I was fishing behind the house, earlier that summer we watched a black bear tear the bird feeder off the front porch, and for several days there were two subadult brown bears feeding on spawning salmon in view of our upstairs bathroom window. Add in the occasional lynx, wolf, fox, great horned owls, and our ubiquitous eagles, and this isn't exactly a pet-safe environment. And even though Ed's close encounter likely involved nothing more exotic than the neighborhood's pugnacious Jack Russell terrier, the cats are no longer allowed outside and thus they spend every waking hour plotting an escape.

In response, I built an elaborate cat-containment chamber off the side door. People often mistake it for a screened porch, but its real purpose is to stop the feline convicts from bolting into the forest every time one of us guards opens the back door. They still bolt out the door, only now they can't get any farther than the screened porch door. Theoretically.

So when my wife came home, arms filled with groceries, junk mail, and a purse the size of a violin case, she held both doors open simultaneously for about two seconds. All the cats needed.

They jumped off the porch and came racing across the snow in my direction, the three younger ones in a phalanx with old fat Ed limping along behind. The young ones raced toward me at the speed of cruising bonefish, so I led them by six feet and cast, setting the hot pink fly down right in front of them. In unison they skidded to a halt on the hard-packed snow and crouched, tails twitching like snakes in a frying pan. Ed came staggering up behind, panting.

I gave the fly a little strip, and the pink feathers hopped across the snow like a mouse wearing its grandmother's hat. The lead cat, Blizzard, a big "flame-point" Siamese with bright orange ears and a freckled nose, pounced so hard he sank through the crust up to his belly. I yanked the fly another foot, and the other three cats jumped all over each other trying to get it. Except Ed. He mostly rolled around like the pinniped he's becoming. Even "the baby" got in a couple pounces as I picked up the fly and laid it back down among them again and again until I had them racing around in circles, snapping their teeth. It's hard to say if cats experience fun in the way we use the word, but I was having a fine time.

Then my wife came out and tried to recapture them. They fled in four directions, leaving her standing in the drifts in her good clothes saying something about the kind of man who would tease house cats with a fly rod. I wasn't listening as closely as I might have been. Fast fishing like that doesn't happen every day—even in Alaska—especially not in winter. It was the best I'd felt in a month. I guess exercise really is good for you.

I hung the rod in the garage and joined my wife, wandering the property, calling the cats by name, thinking that by the time I got back from fishing in Mexico it would be late April. It might still be snowing, of course, but I knew that those last-ditch squalls would be weak and impotent. The mountainous berms created along the driveway by Tim the Snow-Plow Guy would be shrunk to lumpy ridges or maybe gone altogether. The driveway would be a muddy quagmire capable of swallowing a mastodon, but the culverts would ring with the sweet sound of running snowmelt. The willows and alders would be starting to unfurl their sticky buds, the fiddleheads poking through the brown fern remnants in the ravine next to the house. Overhead, the lesser Canada geese would be honking, the sandhill cranes croaking their ridiculous travel song. We would dig clams on the big spring tides and have cocktails on the front deck in the late-afternoon sun, the cats crowded inside against the front-door glass, glaring with resentment.

Eventually it would be time to fish again. May would come, and the river would break up, and the king salmon would return in time for the Memorial Day opener, as always. And when the first bright-orange fillets hit the barbecue grill it would officially be summer in Alaska, and once more I would remember why I live here and I would be happy.

But until then, if anyone wants me I'll be out back behind the shop, standing in snow up to my knees, casting to cats, and wearing my winter face.

PART III

If You Will Permit

CHAPTER 13

Anything but Mercy

I

Maybe it's my Catholic upbringing, but I have this horrible feeling that eventually we will all get exactly what we deserve. That's why I think I must be living someone else's life right now, because today I caught an eight-pound bonefish and met the loveliest female bartender in all of the Bahamas. It is either my third day on Great Abaco Island, or I have actually died and entered heaven using somebody else's ID.

Our host at Rickmon Bonefish Lodge, Ricardo Burrows, has invited my fishing partner Will Rice and me to a local beach picnic this evening after the best day of saltwater fishing we have ever had anywhere. The picnic bar is a large, open-sided wooden pavilion built with green, pressure-treated posts and beams from distant Canada, and money from the Bahamian government's hurricane-relief fund. Here, a few yards from the gently rolling surf in which a large woman, her little boy, and a six-foot lemon shark can be seen lolling about, the Sandy Point chapter of the Anglican Men's Council is selling Kalik brand beer and assorted adult drinks to raise money for all the good works the church does in these islands. The food includes local favorites such as conch fritters and fresh conch salad, fried barracuda fillets, and the ubiquitous Caribbean "peas and rice." For those seeking more international fare, there are corn dogs, burgers, and coleslaw. Although there are at least six perfectly capable-looking Anglican men tending the four-sided pavilion bar, to make absolutely certain that the fund-raising does not lag, the organization has brought in a Bahamian charm machine named Mercy.

Mercy is fair-skinned and soft-eyed, and has a black belt in flirting. I am only halfway through my first drink when she appears at my elbow. "Oh, you been bonefishing with Ricardo all day?" she sings, training her fool-trapping eyes on me. "You must be sooooo thirsty." Somehow she makes the phrase "bonefishing all day," sound like "fighting forest fires all day," or "trekking the Sahara."

I show her my plastic tumbler, still half-filled with rum. She looks hurt. "But it's for such a good cause," she whines. I wonder momentarily how the encouragement of male vanity can in any possible way be described as a good cause. Of course, my ego is swelling like an infected wound now, so I make another contribution to the Anglican Men's Council, pound down the old drink and lurch away from the bar with fresh rum in hand before this woman can stick any more hooks in me. Her mother should have named her Grace, or simply Beauty. Anything but Mercy.

Up and down the beach, the people of Sandy Point are celebrating Easter. There are dozens of children running among the adults standing, eating, and drinking in knots around the various barbecue grills and folding tables covered with platters of fish and chicken. Parked cars and trucks line both shoulders of the cracked two-lane road, their proudly-polished-for-the-picnic finishes glistening in the gorgeous Caribbean sunset. A massive, brand-new Dodge Ram idles mid-road. Teenage boys and girls clamber into its bed, and it lurches off with hilarious giggling from everyone on board, including the young man who is dangling from the tailgate, feet just clearing the pavement beneath them. I'm pleased to see that even here in the Bahamas, on an island that barely clears sea level and lies in the path of every tropical storm of the year, a youthful belief in immortality is alive and well.

Tonight the people of the town are also celebrating the beginning of this year's bonefish season. Nearly all the younger men we meet here are fishing guides. In an uncanny way, they remind me of Japanese airline pilots: all of them are uniformly handsome and fit. They have come to the party in crisp pleated chinos and knit shirts that bulge over biceps and shoulders developed poling skiffs across the several thousand acres of marl and turtle grass flats that hug the lee side of Abaco Island. The guides are pleased to hear we had a good day of fishing, but they tell us that it is just beginning, and that April and May are the peak months. Well, we may be a little early, but that very afternoon we caught fish after fish, wading barefoot in knee-deep water over flawless white sand. Unhooking a twenty-eight-inch bonefish with a girth that taped out at nearly sixteen inches, I laughed out loud when Ricardo said, "In a couple weeks the fishing will be amazing."

Everything about bonefish is amazing: their speed, their wariness, their ability to appear and then vanish in water that doesn't seem deep enough to hide a sardine. And then there is their power when hooked. I've caught hundreds of fish this size on a fly rod—not because I know what I'm doing, but only because I live in Alaska, where salmon number in the tens of millions, and fly fishing for them can be about as challenging as bowhunting for dairy cows. But in the past three days on the Abaco bonefish flats, I've seen sections of my fly line backing that no sockeye, silver, or king salmon has ever exposed before.

Blistering, knuckle-cracking hookups, consistently pretty women, and daylong eighty-degree sunshine make me wonder what the Bahamian residency laws are like. And these people know how to picnic.

Music is blasting from huge plywood speaker cabinets now. Over the late afternoon wind and surf, to my rum-addled ears it sounds like a blend of reggae and hip-hop played underwater. Around the bar, people clutch their drinks and scream into each other's faces about the fishing, the weather, and the government, which, unsurprisingly, is not repairing last year's hurricane damage fast enough to suit them. I glimpse Mercy cruising my way with that "I bet I can sell you another drink" look in her dreamy green eyes, and I turn away from the bar and lurch off into the sea grape bushes to pee before she can harpoon my heart again.

Shakespeare gave the good lines about the quality of mercy to Portia, but he knew enough to dress her up like a man to deliver them. No man wants a lecture on that subject from a woman.

It's going to be a fine party. In the morning we'll fish for bones again.

II

The day dawns virtually windless, a first for me. For years I've studied the photos in magazines in which flats anglers cast tight, unhurried loops over perfectly calm water. But every time I've gone to the tropics there is an "unseasonable" cold front under way; the wind is peeling the bark off the palm trees and the pelicans are wearing earmuffs. Invariably we spend half the week huddled indoors watching the guide's skiffs being blown up onto the beach.

Not today. The air is thick and still under a bloodred sunrise as we stow our rods in Ricardo's boat and set out across flat seas. Will and I are joking about the lovely Mercy and the career in marketing she could have. Ricardo, a very married man and father of eight, just shakes his head. We are not his first clients to succumb to Mercy's charms. Thankfully her boyfriend yanked her from behind the bar early in the evening, so we are operating with only minor morning-after brain poisoning. I look at the windless sky and think about how much trouble those bonefish are in now.

A lot, it turns out. We catch big fish by the hour, including a pair of twenty-nine-inchers that must weigh close to nine pounds apiece. I am casting as well as I ever have—which is to say adequately—and the bones are finding our flies as hard to refuse as Mercy's rum drinks. All is well.

And then we see the first permit.

This trip is my return to flats fishing after a three-year hiatus prompted by several fruitless weeklong attempts to catch a permit, after which I swore I was never setting a fly line in saltwater again. When Will suggested a trip to the Bahamas, my first wary response was, "Not you-know-what." Will said, "Just bonefish. We'll keep a 10-weight rigged with a crab pattern just in case, but the odds are we won't see any . . ." He let it trail off. Wanting to be talked into going, I agreed. Now, just when I had almost forgotten about the "P" word, Ricardo whispers "Permit!" and I find myself scrambling for the heavy rod like a wino at a beer truck crash.

The permit is tailing in two feet of water off the point of a little mangrove island when I get up on the deck and make a "tar baby" cast, wrapping the fly around the rod so intricately that the more I tug and fuss with it the more hopelessly the hook becomes mired in the snarl. By the time I get it straightened out the permit has packed up his tail and darted away. It is a brief encounter, hardly anything at all, and yet I know that everything has changed now. I want to catch a permit sooooo bad.

I put away the permit rod and pretend not to be affected, in much the same way I lay in bed after the picnic last night, saying, "The girl is half your age and has a steady boyfriend. Take a look in the mirror. You are a happily married sub-geezer. Get real." And so forth. In a while, when we start catching bonefish again, I convince myself I'm over the permit incident. But unlike Mercy, who we won't see again, later this day we'll come across another permit that finishes me off.

We are slowly motoring along a deep cut, about to pull up onto another mangrove-dotted flat late in the afternoon, when Ricardo says the dreaded word: "Permit! Permit on that stingray!" He kills the engine and reaches for the boat pole and I'm already closing my trembling fingers around the handle of the permit rod.

The permit is feeding behind a huge stingray in about four feet of water. It is so focused on the food the ray is kicking up that it lets us get within twenty feet of it. I make the first good cast to a permit in my life, dropping the crab pattern right on its nose.

Ricardo says, "Let it sink. Let it sink. Strip, strip."

Nothing.

Ten more casts—one of which briefly foulhooks the ray by the tail and sends it scurrying ahead a hundred feet. More nothing from the permit.

I change flies and Ricardo poles us closer to the fish again.

We are now almost directly over the stingray. The permit still blithely feeds on. I lower a Whisper Crab in front of it, at one point actually setting the pale fly on the dark brown back of the stingray. I watch it slide right off and under the nose of the permit, which rolls its giant eyeball at the hook and keeps right on eating something else.

Bigger crab patterns. Smaller crab patterns. Green crabs. Blue. Tan. Pink.

Nothing.

Shrimp patterns, worm patterns, the whole seafood platter. If I had a fish stick fly I would try that.

Nada.

Finally I sink a Clouser Minnow into the stingray's wing tip. To my horror, the permit tips up and covers the fly with its thick crab-crushing lips but can't dislodge the hook from the leathery skin of the ray. It tries to eat the fly again. The fly does not budge.

Ricardo says, "That's a big permit. Maybe twenty-five pounds. And he really wants that fly."

I can feel the gray hairs multiplying across my head, my chin, my chest. It's like Dorian Grey's tropical vacation photo come to life.

When the stingray has had enough abuse, he powers up his wings and snaps my tippet, and he and the permit are last seen heading in the general direction of Nassau.

I realize that it is impertinent to beseech God with small and selfish matters such as my desire to catch a certain fish, but there comes a time in every permit fisherman's life when he will find himself tempted to beg the big guy Himself for help, pleading for intercession with the fish on his behalf, and petitioning Him to please, please, please just this once make it take the fly. Without actually admitting how many times I've been reduced to that myself, let me just say that it never works.

As we pull up to the lodge that evening, the resident gulls burst into a fit of low tide hilarity and I swear they are looking right at me. I wonder if therapy might help me deal with my permit issues better than it has helped me with any of the other things that have made me the quivering bundle of neuroses I am today.

III

Thankfully, we do not see another permit in the last two days of the trip, and though we are predictably flummoxed by several even more skittish mutton snappers, the muttons have the decency to bolt the minute we come near. There is none of the flirtatious rod-teasing which the taunting permit seem to enjoy, and for that I am truly grateful. No, our third and final lesson on the subject of mercy (or the lack of same) comes on dry land, in a bar in Marsh Harbor where we overnight on our way back to the States.

Marsh Harbor, the largest town on Abaco Island, is a major sailing destination. There are hundreds of boats of every description moored in its extensive marina, and the upscale restaurants are full of well-heeled tourists. After a sumptuous dinner that did not include anything made with conch for the first time in a week, Will and I come across a hopping patio bar, the music suitably overpowering and the room packed with both the middle-aged sailing crowd and young locals. The band consists of three young Bahamian men singing karaoke style over recorded music. One of them has a pair of maracas, which he shakes with terrific energy. But the music is so loud the maracas may be empty for all I can tell. I think back to my own brief career as a young barroom musician and kick myself for wasting all that time learning to play an instrument. Still, the buoyant pop-reggae is irresistible. In we go.

We nestle in amid the scruffy fly fishermen and sailing bums loitering near the bar. There are a handful of overweight, red-faced guys wearing flowered shirts who have either failed to notice, or simply don't care, that since they first fell in love with him thirty years ago, Jimmy Buffett—that icon of free-wheeling tropical adventure—has become an overweight, red-faced restaurant franchiser in a flowered shirt. Seated at the best tables are upscale boating types, looking splendid in resort wear and nuclear tans. They tend to be couples in Dockers, or families with prepubescent girls sipping soft drinks and playing with their blond kiddie-dreads.

The local Bahamians are almost all twenty-somethings. Pretty women, coifed and dressed way too grandly for a simple night out at a bar, are lined up against a wall looking like they are waiting for a bus to take them someplace a lot nicer. Their male counterparts have shown up dressed as NBA stars. Shiny nylon shorts and numbered shirts, cell phones, and gold bling are the uniform of the day. The girls lean into the wall looking bored, and the guys mill around, trading handshakes or talking on cell phones. Nobody is dancing until a couple suddenly materializes directly in front of the blaring speaker columns. Things get interesting.

The woman is a tourist, fortyish, blond and tall and thin and straight off a boat I will never be able to afford. She has a long patrician face and is as aloof as a mutton snapper, barely acknowledging the existence of the room around her as she dances. Her partner is one of the young local guys in a shiny Lakers outfit. They are "freak" dancing.

Freak dancing is a term I know only because my wife is a high school counselor and it is the latest weapon teenagers have deployed in their never-ending quest to horrify their elders. Basically it is simulated copulation done standing up and to music. Until now I had dismissed the uproar it was causing at school dances, arguing that in our day we scandalized our folks with the Twist and the Shimmy. I believed it was the way kids said to their parents and teachers, "Imagine what we are doing when you are not around." I see now that freak dancing totally eliminates the need for an imagination.

This woman is a heck of a freak dancer. She is lithe and fit and moves very well, in spite of the fact that she and her dancing partner have apparently spilled super-glue on their laps, which are now securely pressed together. The front of the kid's official NBA shorts is tight against the white chino fabric of her capri pants, and as they hop up and down to the music there is enough friction to make me understand why prom committees everywhere are sweating.

Still, they are both adults. Even if she is old enough to be his mother, it's none of my business. It *is*, however, the business of her husband who is sitting at a nearby table with another similarly dressed yachting couple and the empty chair where his wife should be. From time to time she glances his way to see if he is suffering satisfactorily. He is. She closes her eyes and pushes against her young partner a little harder. The husband stares down into his drink, probably deciding whether to crawl to the dance floor and beg for mercy or simply kill himself with his swizzle stick.

The band has flipped the playback machine into autorepeat and the exuberant music goes on forever, with the singers joyfully repeating the refrain, "Woozy Suzy, Woozy Suzy, Woozy Suzy!" over and over and over. I don't know if this is a venerable Bahamian song or just something they made up for the occasion, but it goes on for another five minutes or so before the woman's husband finally stands and storms out of the room. A satisfied smile crosses her face. She keeps on dancing. The kid presses against her a little harder.

I look at Will and he shrugs. "Kinda makes you wonder what her husband did to piss her off like that," he shouts over the music.

I watch the woman brace herself with one hand on an aluminum pole that supports the canvas roof over the dance floor. She lifts her left leg and wraps it around the young man's hip. He reaches behind his back and clutches her ankle and holds it there and presses further into her groin. Locked together that way, they continue hopping up and down to the beat of "Woozy Suzy."

"I wonder," I say.

Ultimately a drunk fifty-something tourist with a ponytail and his ball cap yanked around backwards decides it is all too much. He grabs the dancing kid by the shoulder and tries to cut in. The kid looks up, bleary-eyed and startled. There is some shouting and finger waving. He drops the woman's leg and grabs a beer bottle off the nearest table and swings. But a group of the basketball guys dive on their young friend before he can connect with the staggering American geezer. They hustle the kid out of the place before it goes any further, aware that—no matter who started it—a homey who hits a tourist with a bottle is going to be the one who spends the night in the slammer.

Declining the drunk's attempts at joining her, the woman stands there solo now, still writhing to the music until her husband suddenly pops back in and grabs her by the wrist. As they wind their way out through the tables, the crowd cheers and the band plays on. Woozy Suzy, Woozy Suzy, Woozy Suzy, Woozy Suzy!

The woman smiles broadly, triumphant now, confident in her abilities—the way I felt after a day of catching bonefish at Sandy Point. Her husband, on the other hand, has the haunted and thoroughly defeated look of a man who has spent the day casting to permit.

Chapter 14

Adiós, Señor Permit

I don't actually speak Spanish, but since a school of Mexican permit precipitated a life-changing decision for me, I think I should wish them well in their native tongue. That said, I never want to see another member of their species for as long as I live.

I cast to my first permit in 1996, and in all the years since then, after all the long fights from Alaska to the Caribbean, after all the world-class guides and all the rum drink hangovers and all the monster VISA bills, I have not had one single permit take a fly I cast to it. Not one. None. Nada.

I've tried for them in Ascension Bay, South Water Cay of Belize, Little Cayman Island, Abaco Island in the Bahamas, and, finally, Chetumal Bay near Xcalak, on the southernmost tip of the Yucatán Peninsula, where—after casting to so many uncooperative permit in one day I lost count—I witnessed an entire gang of the miserable bastards actually fighting over my fishing partner's fly. Then and there I realized that this kind of abuse at the fins of a fish cannot be good for a person.

And I quit.

I'm a fairly competent trout angler, as long as the trout themselves are fairly incompetent, and I catch a goodly number of salmon on flies here in Alaska where the salmon are as thick as, well, flies. I have had a few good days catching bonefish—when they were both as thick as flies and incompetent. And, I even catch steelhead with some regularity, a species responsible for gray hairs of frustration on the heads of much better fishermen than I. So, why would I travel halfway to the Equator only to be humiliated by permit? There are probably drugs that produce the same cycle of momentary excitement and subsequent self-loathing that permit fishing does, and I don't do those either.

It has been five years since I have even seen a permit, and the recurring nightmares about casting behind them, beyond them, short of them, hitting one in the side of the head with a weighted crab pattern, and so forth have tapered off now. Rarely do I awake bathed in sweat any more, the words, *"Señor! That was the most worst cast of the whole week!"* ringing in my ears. It's been nice.

The last time I fished for permit was in April 2006, when I spent a week with Will Rice, writer, photographer, and old friend, at the wonderful Costa de Cocos Lodge near the village of Xcalak, Mexico, a five-hour drive south of Cancún and a short cast from the border with Belize. When we arrived at the little thatch-roofed resort, a half-dozen Idaho trout bums were just finishing their stay, sunburned and a little delirious—not just from the Caribbean sun or the drinks in the breezy Cocos seaside bar, but from the three flats fishing "grand slams" they had gotten while there. Three! In three consecutive days. Although the Yucatán's "Coconut Coast" and Chetumal Bay are perhaps the richest permit waters in Mexico, even the Costa de Cocos Lodge owners, Ilana and David Randall, had to admit they had never seen that done before.

The last time I had been in camp when an angler caught a bonefish, a tarpon, and a permit all in the same day was at Casa Blanca

Lodge in Ascension Bay, in 1996. I still remember the celebration, the guide Pedro's gold tooth flashing in the evening sun as he grinned over the rim of a Cuba Libre and saluted his lucky sport. I also remember being insanely jealous of the angler, who was such a likable guy I had to forgive him not only for being a wealthy Texan, but for being a superb flats fisherman on top of it. It was my first attempt at saltwater fly fishing. I told myself I would get better at it. I told myself that next time I would catch a permit.

I was still hoping for my first one, ten years later, as I sat at the bar in Cocos with Will, listening to those Idaho sports recount the glory of each particular grand slam. I pounded down large margaritas and squinted at them, imagining each of them with the head of a farm animal in place of his own. (It was not as satisfying as you would think.) Like the Texan at Casa Blanca, these guys were also self-effacing and charming and maddeningly impossible to dislike. Listening to them, I realized that one day when I finally enter my own customized level of hell, it will be a bar filled with every person who has ever caught a permit on a fly. Anywhere. Each angler will be as friendly and likable as the next. I will spend my days listening to them describe, in the kind of detail only eternity allows, permit after permit after permit. Satan will serve me only alcohol-free chardonnay.

When the Idaho fishermen departed Cocos in the morning, there were no other anglers left in camp beside Will and me. So, Ilana and David, wanting to keep their four guides employed equitably, asked us if we would be interested in rotating through the lineup for a couple days instead of fishing with one guide for our entire stay. This was a place where three grand slams had just been recorded. Yes, we would fish with a different guide each day. I would have agreed to fish with one of the nice old women from the kitchen.

True, it can be a real pleasure to spend a whole week with one guide. You develop a vocabulary of grunts and signs that say all that needs to be said when the fish are there. Sometimes—when the fish are not there—you even find yourself talking about things unrelated to fishing, and your relationship feels more like a friendship than a business arrangement. I would not trade anything for the many hours spent sitting in a panga talking with Belizean legend Lincoln Westby, or sharing an anisette with him at the end of the day in his tiny wooden lodge on stilts on his tiny mangrove island. And after a week of huge bonefish and even bigger laughs with the delightful Ricardo Burrows on Abaco Island, I thought I had discovered a Bahamian half-brother my mother neglected to tell me about.

But think about this: A guide who has only one day to prove himself will fish like there is no tomorrow. He wants it to be good, very good. And he will do what it takes to make that happen. I was in one of the best places in the world to catch a permit, apparently at the peak of the season, and about to fish with a bevy of highly motivated guides. I had not yet articulated the idea that if I failed here, under these conditions, I might as well give up. But I think it was beginning to percolate on the back burner of my brain.

Our first guide was Alejandro.

In Mexico, many of the guides grew up on the waters where they work, and each has his own proven methods. Alejandro loved wading, and we were happy to hear that. It was April, still early spring, which in Alaska means winter. Walking around in warm water in a bathing suit would be fine with me even if we were not fishing. There is also something more exciting about sneaking up on a fish on foot than standing on the casting deck of a flats boat being poled around all day like a tourist in a Venetian gondola.

Yet wading can create logistical problems. If the guide anchors or beaches the boat so you can wade alongside him, you are going to have to walk back through the spooked water to return to the boat. The farther you wade away from the boat, the longer the walk back. That means a lot of time not fishing. Or it means that one angler must bring the boat along while his partner is wading and fishing with the guide. Either way, somebody is missing out on fishing time.

But Alejandro had a secret weapon: his ten-year-old son and apprentice, Jonah. With young Jonah following a couple hundred feet behind us pushing the boat, Will and Alejandro and I waded for hours that first day.

Alejandro was not a hardcore permit guide like some. Maybe that was a good thing. I was so wound up about the probability of breaking my permit jinx, the last thing I needed was a fanatic egging me on. I had suffered so many ignominious refusals from permit, ruined so many opportunities over the years. I was practically twitching with concern that when I did run into the prolific hordes of them alleged to be there in Chetumal Bay I would blow the chance yet again and try to beat myself to death with the boat anchor. I needed to relax a little and enjoy the fabulous country and the beautiful water and stop thinking about permit for a few seconds.

Thank God for bonefish.

There is nothing like catching fish to take your mind off worrying about not catching fish. For the first two hours of the day, we stood in one spot in a mud-bottomed bay sinking up to our calves in the muck, picking bonefish off as they came in with the tide. A few days later, we were in the bar with a newly arrived sport who complained to us over drinks about the deep mud Alejandro had made him endure. He said he'd put a stop to that and made Alejandro take him back to a well-known and very heavily fished sand spit at nearby Punta Maya. He also complained about not catching too many fish there. Will and I looked at each other. He said, "Yeah. There's a lot of mud in some places."

Not all of Alejandro's favorite places were muddy bonefish holes. Late in the afternoon, Will and I were wading with him along the edge of a white sandy cove nearby the deep cut of water that connected the Caribbean and the Bay of Chetumal when he spotted the scissor tails of permit in the surf line a short distance down the beach. They were coming our way. He motioned for everyone to freeze.

I clipped off the bonefish fly and tied on a crab pattern. "Two of them," Alejandro said, when the tails jutted out of the surface again, much closer to us this time. Will was not in a position to cast to them, so Alejandro told me where to put the fly and for once I managed to do it right. The permit saw it sinking through the water column and swam over to investigate. Perfect. Here were a pair of permit, feeding actively in two feet of water over a pure white bottom. For about thirty seconds, I almost believed it was going to work. And why not? Those guys from Idaho were tailwater trout anglers, for chrissake! We're talking 3-weight rods and flies the size of subatomic particles. If those sissies could catch permit, how hard could it be?

It was virtually a done deal. I was already thinking about going to the tarpon lagoon to round out my grand slam. The permit examined the crab pattern with their giant eyeballs and apparently found it to be the most terrifying thing they had ever encountered. They nearly swam over us in their panic to get away from it. They were the only permit we saw that afternoon.

Later, while Will was taking care of business with Alejandro at the lodge, I found little Jonah down at the water cleaning his father's boat. He was pleased to get his own personal tip. I could almost see him calculating how long it would take to buy a boat of his own. I wanted to say to him, "Son, don't grow up to be a permit guide." But I knew he would not listen—even if I could speak Spanish.

Evilio was our guide the next day.

He went by Evie, but around the lodge they called him Rasta for his bountiful dreadlocks. He said he was from the northern part of Mexico, and unlike the uniformly diminutive locals with their Mayan ancestry, he was tall and thin—more European looking than Central American. He was probably the youngest of the four guides we met that week, and the most modern. He was also very handsome and spoke excellent English. I got the feeling he had never met a woman he didn't like—or vice versa.

Evie was adventurous and liked to explore, looking for fish. He took us deep into a tarpon lagoon by way of a creek barely wide enough for the boat to fit through, and as far north up into Chetumal Bay as we ventured the whole time we were there. He was more willing to experiment than the others who had their favorite methods and stuck to them, and he mixed the day equally between wading and poling. His flexible tastes extended to what we fished for as well. Like Alejandro, Evilio was not obsessed with permit. He just wanted us to catch fish. And, in spite of an unfortunate cold front moving in, he got us into the biggest bonefish of the week, including a couple over five pounds—which are pretty good bones for the Yucatán.

We did not catch much that day, and did not see any permit at all. But, between the two of us, Will and I have lived and fished in Alaska for nearly sixty years. As a result, we are both grateful for every minute of Caribbean sun that lands on our increasingly balding heads, regardless of how slow the fishing is. Still, the falling barometer took its toll on the fishing. A couple of big bonefish aside, this was a very slow day indeed. As it turned out, Evie was the perfect guy to be in a boat with during the long fishless hours.

Some Mexican guides seem to be taciturn, even unfriendly, obsessed with finding fish. But I think that is more likely because we do not speak Spanish than any unfriendliness on their part. Perhaps because of Evie's fluency with English, he was a terrific talker, and he turned out to be knowledgeable not just about the fish, but the flora and fauna of the area too. When he discovered we had a passing interest in birds, he took us to a wood stork sanctuary where the Mexican government, beginning to see the dollar signs in ecotourism, had erected a three-story wooden viewing tower on pilings a short distance from a rookery island. From the platform on top, we could see the huge storks gliding to and from their nests in the dense mangrove forest blanketing the island. Wood storks have enormous wingspans and long scimitar beaks curving down slightly at the tip, giving them a prehistoric, vaguely reptilian appearance. Standing up there in the moist jungle heat, I found myself expecting to see a tyrannosaurus, or maybe King Kong, leap up out of the foliage and snatch one from the sky. I'll admit I watch too many movies.

Later Evie showed us a weird daisy chain of saltwater catfish: thousands of them swimming, nose to tail, in a slow circle, fifty feet in diameter in knee-deep water. Not that he was not interested in the fishing. Of all the guides, he was most absorbed in the gear and was very particular about knots, and an expert at tying complex tarpon leaders. Later in the week, I watched each morning as Evie prepared to guide other newly arriving sports. He was always the first person on the dock at dawn, checking leaders and examining fly boxes.

Maybe because he was a little younger than the others and had lived in other places and spoke other languages, he was also the most ambitious. He told us about a trout lodge in the mountains of Chile he had an interest in, and showed us photos of sports holding up tarpon the size of walruses from a place where he guided off the northern Yucatán island of Holbox. With his cell phone and his business cards and his relaxed charm, Evilio was clearly a man with his eyes on the future. I wish him luck.

Our third guide was Beto. Unlike the first two, Beto was intent on catching permit. But, unfortunately, as the cold front continued, he drew a day of high winds and crashing barometric pressure. The palms around the lodge were nearly prostrate on the sand as Will and I walked to the wind-racked dock with our rods. We watched the frigate birds overhead pitching in the gale and the furiously spinning blades on the big windmill that—along with solar panels and a huge generator—provides some of the twenty-four-hour electricity at the lodge. Beyond the reef, the horizon was saw-toothed with open sea waves. We weren't too optimistic, but Beto fired up the Yamaha outboard and set off, oblivious to the whitecaps we began slamming through. We got a little relief motoring through the mangrove-lined cut and past the Mexican Coast Guard outpost. But when we came out into the huge Chetumal Bay, the gusts were shearing the tips off the waves again.

Still, a Caribbean guide who did not know how to fish in wind would soon be pumping gas in a Pemex station on dry land. Beto pushed on and took us to a stretch of relatively sheltered shoreline where we immediately got a couple shots at predictably finicky permit. Clearly unhappy with the refusals, Beto asked to see our fly boxes. Unlike most permit guides I had fished with, he did not think much of crab patterns.

"Mantis shrimp?" he asked.

I opened my fly box. He selected the only thing I had remotely mantis-like and nodded. His reasoning was that the real crabs that permit feed on do not move much, and certainly not when threatened by a predator; to survive, they depend upon protective coloration, not speed. If you strip a crab pattern across the bottom, it actually alerts the permit that something is unnatural about it. Even if you let a crab fly sink all the way to the bottom and let it lie there motionless, the wave action tugging on the line will move it. Or the fly might hang up on grass or coral, immediately spooking the super fussy permit. A live mantis shrimp, on the other hand, is a more naturally mobile creature that will dart and swim, making it easier to simulate by stripping. Beto explained all that in fair English and was obviously convinced of the logic in it. I liked the sound of it too—mostly because those guys from Idaho had caught all three of their grand slam permit on mantis shrimp patterns.

Not surprisingly, the cold front had cooled the permit action and the fish were making themselves scarce that morning, so we didn't get a good chance to test his theory again that day. But that mantis fly worked very well on bonefish, and it got me perhaps my most memorable fish in ten years of saltwater fishing. Not a permit, of course, but still.

We had stopped in the lee of an island to have lunch, and Beto prepared to beach the boat. There we came upon a reddish heron wading in the shallows, and Will asked me to get out of the boat and wade as close to it as I could get for a photo op: a guy and a bird fishing together. The heron, being nearly four feet tall and armed with a needle-pointed bill, probably had few natural predators to worry about. It let me get extremely close as Will photographed madly and directed me to move this way or that.

Following his directions, I lifted my fly rod to pose, simulating a moment in which I had apparently spotted a fish and was about to cast to it. But, while in that fake casting position I was astounded to actually see a real bonefish swimming toward me parallel to the shore about three rod lengths away. I laid the mantis shrimp in front of it, stripped a few times and the fish inhaled it and tried to rip the rod out of my hands. While I played the bonefish into the shallows at my feet, the unflappable reddish heron never moved. Will took the last picture of me releasing the fish with the bird practically looking over my shoulder. Beto could not understand what we found so remarkable about any of this. It was just another bonefish to him, another wading bird. He was itching to eat lunch and go find permit.

Beto was also smart enough to know when it was time to change tactics. That afternoon when we ran out of protected shoreline and the wind kicked up so hard he could barely stay upright while polling the boat, he gave up and set the anchor off the transom, upwind of a huge mud plume created by a school of stingrays. In the patches of clear water between the slurries of gray silt kicked up by the rays, groups of bonefish would suddenly appear, feeding on whatever had gotten kicked up. Will and I took turns making long casts out to the feeding fish, the howling wind blasting over our shoulders. Trying to punch our backcasts into that gale was arm wrenching and not nearly as enjoyable as sneaking up on a fish in the shallows. But we caught some fair-sized bones that way. It was a fun day, all in all, and most importantly I was beginning to think I might have put the whole permit thing in perspective. What was so special about permit, anyway? Maybe I was over my fixation.

The next morning, I met Fernando, and whatever remnants of proportion or balance I briefly thought I might still possess evaporated in the warm Caribbean air. Fernando's desire to catch permit made mine look like a whim. He was either just an average guy who was lucky enough to be at the helm on April 16, 2006, when possibly every permit in Chetumal Bay decided to reveal itself to us, or he's some kind of genius. Dickens would have said it was the best of permit days; it was the worst of permit days. Ever. I have never seen so many in one place in my life. And I never will again. Because, after this day, I quit.

We must have seen a hundred permit before noon. All morning as Fernando poled the boat, Will and I took turns casting to singles, doubles, schools of six or eight fish who, in typical permit fashion, would not touch a hook, even one cleverly disguised as a mantis shrimp. Every refusal was frustrating, but every new sighting erased that frustration and sent my heart flip-flopping with hope again. And I would cast, foolishly believing yet again that the permit would fall for my trickery. Of course, they did not. But, as I said, their constant maddening refusals are *not* why I quit fishing for them forever.

This is why I quit fishing for them forever.

About midday, Will was up on the casting deck as Fernando poled us along the lee side of the mainland, hugging the shore, trying to stay out of the ferocious windstorm. Suddenly Fernando, yet again, said, "Permit." Only this time there was a strange new excitement in his voice. "Big school!" he said. "Ten o'clock. A hundred feet, maybe more. Coming straight at us! Look! Look! Beeeeeg fish!"

"Big school" was right, and so was "Big fish." Even *I* could see them, and my fish-spotting skills are only slightly less laughable than my investment acumen and my dance moves. Most of the permit we had seen all week had been typical small fish, less than ten pounds. But Fernando was not kidding about these monsters. A huge school of enormous permit was coming up out of the deep green open water on our left and onto the shallow flat, obviously hunting for food. Beeeeeg fish!

I don't know how many there were altogether: I had my eyes on the leaders, but I could see that many more were swarming in behind them. When Will cast his fly into a patch of water over a white sand bottom ten feet ahead of the school, the front five or six permit started climbing over each other to get to it. Their broad backs actually came out of the surface, sickle-shaped dorsals and pointy tails glittering in the sunlight as the huge fish lunged for the fly.

It's hard to convey how it felt to see numerous permit actually racing *toward* a fly instead of away from it. For most of a decade I had been watching them act as though they found my flies either mildly repulsive or something to flee from. Now, a whole pod of trophy-sized specimens was fighting for the privilege of eating my fishing partner's fly right before my eyes.

When one of the permit ate Will's fly, I don't know who was more surprised—the fish or me. It realized its mistake and went nuts, crashing back into the rest of the school, and the surface of the water erupted in a foaming maelstrom, as maybe fifty gigantic permit panicked and blasted off in every direction, crisscrossing the surface like frenzied bonitos.

Will stood there, as awestruck as I was, as the backing spooled off his reel and vanished through the rod guides and the hooked fish headed for the far side of Chetumal Bay. I grabbed his camera and got a shaky photo of the fiercely bent rod, the white backing flossing the green waves, Will's happy, astounded face. Unfortunately, the next couple photos were of the suddenly straight rod, the suddenly limp line, and Will's considerably less happy face. He reeled in and grimaced at the sight of the suddenly shortened tippet. "Well," he said, capturing my thoughts precisely, "*that's* never going to happen again, is it?"

I had to agree the odds were exceedingly small that we would ever see that many permit that size attack a hook with feathers and yarn tied to it. What on earth were all those big deepwater fish doing together in a school, feeding in three feet of water a few yards from the beach? I will see those broad-shouldered monsters coasting into that patch of white sand for the rest of my life, that explosion of water and enormous fish. And so will Will. The difference is that each time he sees that moment he will want to grab his bags and head for the Caribbean. I, on the other hand, will remember why I do not.

Fernando was less interested in such distinctions. He looked at the broken leader, shaking his head. Then he stowed the push pole and yanked the starter chord. "I have another place where many permit bite good too, sometimes," he said. But, as he put the outboard in gear, he looked at me and said rather worriedly, "You want to fish for more permit, yes?"

I smiled and nodded. Yes.

But what I was thinking was, *No. Por favor.*

No más.

No más.

No más.

Chapter 15

The Man Who Mistook His Vacation for a Fishing Trip

One summer morning when I was a kid, my mother drove my dad to his job at Great Lakes Carbon Corporation and kept the car for the day. Like most of the women of that time, she did not work outside the home, and so, keys to the car in hand, she packed my numerous younger brothers and sisters and me into the old two-door and drove us to Beaver Island State Park on the shore of the West Niagara River for a day at the beach. I, being eleven years old and male, stupidly brought my fishing tackle along.

At Beaver Island, I helped my mother unload the sand pails and towels, the lunch basket and thermos of lemonade. I helped drag my squirming siblings from the parking lot to the beach. Then, with the little kids happily splashing in the shallows and my mother (apparently also happily) sitting on the beach blanket watching them throw sand in each other's eyes, I took my pushbutton spinning rig and headed for the swampy creek flowing into the big river a quarter mile away. There I spent a memorable afternoon, lobbing a frog-spotted Arbogast Jitterbug into pockets of open water among the lily pads, convinced that there were bass or pike or perhaps even ferocious muskies lurking there. It was a memorable afternoon, not because I caught memorable fish—I did not catch fish of any kind—but because, at some point late in the day, as I stood there in my wet sneakers, still obliviously casting into the fishless swamp, my furious mother stalked up to me and barked, "You've been gone for three hours!"

The mistake I had so foolishly made, of course, was confusing a family outing for a fishing trip. Now I understand that those two things are categorically different experiences, and that no attempts should ever be made to blend the two. I think all grown men know this. And yet, whenever and wherever a family vacation intersects with water, guys who fish keep making that same mistake time and again.

The problem with trying to blend those two very different things is that you can't really put the effort needed into either one of them. Yes, your wife looks happy enough when you leave her at six in the morning, still asleep in a cheap Bahamian motel room so far off the tourist path that the pelicans haven't learned to beg yet. But think about it: she is sleeping. The chances of her maintaining that level of bliss after being awake for six or seven hours in the same very small, not very well air-conditioned motel room are the same as the chances of you catching a bonefish on your own by wandering around knee deep in mud all day trying to figure out which side of the tide to fish. The probability of this all working out to be simply one of those minor vacation setbacks you will both laugh about for years to come is statistically nonexistent.

Anyone can spend a vacation in a strange, foreign place wandering around, more or less lost and uninformed, and still feel privileged simply to be there enjoying himself while *on vacation*. But an actual fishing trip requires, well . . . fish. And in a strange new place, you need a guide and a lot of time to get those fish. You could try to get by on the cheap, try to work a little fishing into your family vacation and do it yourself, unguided. Right?

I'm just going to say it once more: Don't do it. Ever.

But I know you will. So, here are three things you need to remember in order to salvage some semblance of pleasure from it—meaning, of course, catching some fish. (About making the wife happy while doing it? I haven't a clue.)

1. Fish where the locals fish.
2. Fish how the locals fish.
3. Fish when the locals fish.

This should be a no-brainer. Yet, in spite of the fact that I have been making this mistake since I was in sixth grade and should know better, I keep doing it. That brings me to Australia.

RULE NUMBER ONE: FISH WHERE THE LOCALS FISH

In the summer of 2006, my wife, Lin, and I made our second trip to Australia. Five years earlier we had rented a camper and driven for several thousand kilometers across the Northern Territory through a lot of very dry land; I never took my 8-weight rod out of its tube the whole way. This time we were driving the western coastline from north to south, on a road paralleling the Indian Ocean. At home in Alaska we studied the maps, the photos of tropical beaches. My wife saw sand. I saw water, lots of it. And we all know what lives in water. Everything indicated the whole west coast of the continent was an angler's paradise. A vacation/fishing trip on the Indian Ocean!

I know. I know.

We landed in the steaming northwestern Australian town of Broome and picked up the well-used Toyota camper that would be our home for the next month. It was June, summer solstice back at home in Alaska, but winter there in the southern hemisphere where they do everything backwards—including going north to warm up. Broome's latitude is 18 degrees south: about the same distance from the equator as Ambergris Caye in Belize. There were thousands of Aussies from the cold southern cities of Perth, Adelaide, and Melbourne on holiday up on the tropical northern beaches. The once dangerous nineteenth-century pearling port is fast becoming the Key West of Australia, and the similarities with Florida are striking: relentless sunshine, palm trees, peeling tourists, and man-eating reptiles born to become handbags and belts. Signs along Broome's famous Cable Beach warn of dangerous saltwater crocodiles. And what do crocodiles eat? Fish. Well, mostly.

As if to support my theory, a pickup drove past the camper rental place towing a boat bristling with fishing rods. That should have been encouraging, but the boat and the heavy saltwater rods threw a shadow of doubt over my plans to wade around in the shallows casting a fly. Not the least reason being the crocodiles. I decided to keep the fly rod in its case until I got a little more information.

Driving on the left side of the road in that herky-jerky way Americans do for the first week or so at the wheel of British-style vehicles, I managed to grind my way out of town and south to the Broome Bird Observatory. There we would spend a few days in a wonderful campground in a shady jungle grove just across a red sand road from the Indian Ocean. It is a bird watcher's paradise, and I did enjoy the birds. But that was an ocean right there, and what do oceans have in them? Yes.

Yet, squinting through the afternoon sun at the beach, I couldn't help noticing that nobody was fishing. I told myself that was because of the blast furnace afternoon heat, not large reptiles. No one in the campground seemed to know about the fishing there. They were happy to talk about crocodiles, however. I popped the top off a can of the bitter yellow beer they drink down under and struck up a conversation with the nice people in the next site. Somehow, they got the idea my wife and I were Canadians. This would happen everywhere we went for the next month. We would drive more than three thousand kilometers on this trip and would not meet one single American tourist until we got to the big city of Perth. Most of the rangers at the more remote camper parks would tell us we were the first Yanks they had seen in as long as they could remember—if we could even convince them we were Americans. As for Alaskans? Few people there had ever met one before.

We tried to explain that Alaska is, in fact, part of the United States. But it was a tough sell and I soon decided that appearing to be Canadian was not so bad. When I mentioned fishing, somehow the conversation turned to crocodiles. I must have looked sufficiently terrified. Our neighbors reassured me by saying, "No worries, mate! Crocs only eat *Americans*! That's why the attacks are so rare!"

"Ha." I looked down into my beer and I said, "Only eat Americans, eh?"

Crocodiles are considered to be among the canniest predators on earth, actually planning their approach to a victim. We were told not to take the same path to the water more than twice. The Australian crocs favor brackish estuaries and shallow inshore waters—the kinds of places fly fisherman like to wade. But at least there were no box jellyfish, the scourge of Australia's much more populous and popular eastern seaboard, a few thousand kilometers away. I don't know which is scarier: a lizard that plots your death, or a brainless invertebrate that simply floats along in the current maiming anything it bumps into. But that's an Australian day at the beach. Even the enticing tide pools harbor poisonous blue-ringed octopi and the venomous, sculpin-like stonefish—with deadly spines that you never, ever, want to step on. When the talk turned to murderous tiderips and razor sharp coral heads, venomous sea snakes, stingrays, and, of course, Australia's infamous sharks, I decided maybe I'd wait and see if anyone else fished on this beach.

The next morning I got up before the sun was too hot, left Lin already sweltering in the camper bed, and walked to the beach with my fly rod. There wasn't a person in sight for a mile in either direction. I stayed back a yard from the densely blue Indian Ocean and started casting off a sandy spit near enough to the campground that someone might hear my screams. There was not a whisper of wind, and when the sun rose fully, the red sand and red layered rocks of the beach became an oven. I kept casting, sipped on my water bottle, and wondered how large a chunk of my body our insurance company would require my wife to produce before paying the death benefits to her. I also wondered why no one else was fishing.

Soon two battered cars sped past on the sandy road kicking up little cyclones of red dust. They drove to a long rocky point a mile down the beach to my left. A group of dark forms got out and walked to the water and began fishing, or something that looked sort of like fishing.

I thought about Rule Number One: Fish Where the Locals Fish. I started walking.

I tried to walk on the hard-packed sand along the water's edge, but rock piles drove me inland time and again and I wallowed up to my ankles through hot sand. By the time I neared the point where the people were, I was gasping. I was also halfway through my water bottle and a mile from the campground.

As I got closer, something looked odd about the posture of the fishermen. They were sitting down on the sand right at the water's edge, waving their hands in the air over their heads from time to time. This reassured me that there were no crocodiles nearby, but mystified me too. It was not until I was within a hundred feet of them that I realized they were handlining.

The fishermen were local Aboriginal people. There seemed to be several generations of at least two families. The older people, men and women, were doing the actual fishing, while the younger adults were busy taking care of some toddlers who played in the sand and ran back and forth to the vehicles for toys or food or drinks.

I walked up until I was what I hoped a respectable distance away from one older woman. She baited her hook and twirled the weighted end of her line over her head and let it fly. In her left hand she held a tin can around which the line was wrapped. She pointed the bottom of the can at the sea, and the line peeled off and the baited hook and sinker sailed out into the water farther than I can cast with a fly rod. Two men of a similar age were sitting beyond her pinching their lines between thumbs and fingers, waiting for a nibble. I said hello and they all nodded. I took a long pull on what little water I had left. When I started false casting to lay out some line, I thought I heard a snicker, but I did not look.

Under the blasting sun, I lasted about twenty minutes before I concluded that if the locals were not catching fish on bait, chances of me catching anything on a fly were not good when I did not even know what kind of fish I was fishing for or what they ate. I headed back to camp. I have a feeling that somewhere in Northwest Australia, a nice old lady is still telling the story about the crazy white man walking a kilometer under the hot sun just to whip his fishing pole over the water for a few minutes and then walk all the way back to where he came from. I'll bet she cracks them up with that one every time.

Our destination was the city of Perth about eighteen hundred kilometers of two-lane road to the south of Broome. However, the actual coastline of the state of Western Australia is more like twenty thousand kilometers. So the problem of not knowing where to fish was no small matter. To put it in perspective, as we headed south, the next notable point on the map was called the Eighty Mile Beach. Eighty miles. Apparently whoever named it decided to eschew the metric system, maybe because the One Hundred and Twenty-Eight Kilometer Beach would sound absurd. On the map I could see that there was an access road at each end and nothing in between them but sand and water. I asked a young guy at the gas station if that would be a good place for a guy without a boat to do a little fishing. He said, "If you like sharks."

RULE NUMBER TWO: FISH HOW THE LOCALS FISH

We decided not to sample the charms of eighty miles of shark infested waters, and instead arrived in Port Smith late in the afternoon, driving a couple hundred kilometers and enjoying the camper's air-conditioning during the worst heat of the day. At the campground there, I noticed signs of anglers all around, although nothing resembling fly fishing, of course. Thick spinning rods of unimaginable length leaned against the sides of campers; the talismanic word BAIT beckoned from above the door of the campground office as if to say, "Here There Be Fishing."

We found a site and had just set out the camp chairs and reached for the plastic travel cocktail glasses when, with typical Australian friendliness, the people in the next site (Ivan and Shirley) insisted we join them and what turned out to be about a hundred other campers, at a barbecue being held to raise funds for the Western Australia Royal Flying Doctor Service. That is a volunteer cadre of doctors, who, as the name suggests, fly out to the remote towns in the huge empty areas of this territory where there are no hospitals. Being Alaskans—in spite of what the Australians seemed to think—we were familiar with the need for medical care in isolated villages. We agreed to join Ivan and Shirley. I would reconnoiter the fishing prospects and ply the partygoers for info.

For four dollars each, we got a hamburger and a bowl of delicious pumpkin soup, a standard at all Australian dinners in their winter months. Everyone brought their own spoons and chairs, and their own bottles of beer or wine. There was a lot of laughter and lots of yelling—another Australian trait. They are not only some of the friendliest people on the planet, but must rank among the loudest too.

I decided to blend in as best I could to get the skinny on the fishing around there. In order to fish like a local you have to act like a local, right? So I ate like a local. The burgers were pretty much what you would expect in a big country that raises cattle: huge and tasty. What I found most interesting was the condiment table. Along with old standbys like ketchup and mustard and relishes, lettuce, pickles and onions, the Aussies were heaping on shredded carrots and slices of pickled beets—both of which were pretty good. But my hands-down favorite was the extremely well-done fried egg. You have to love a place where the cholesterol in beef is found to be so insubstantial that a fried egg is added for a little extra oomph. I may not be up to crocodiles, but I'm not afraid to live dangerously in order to get fishing information. At my request, the cook hesitantly draped an egg across the top of my burger as if she thought I was going to back out of this at the last second. When I took a big bite for her benefit, she bellowed to the crowd, "Look, the Canadian's having an egg!"

There was more yelling. When a woman dared me to stick around for the karaoke contest, I said, "No, you'll make fun of my American accent."

"American?" she screamed. She slid into an exaggerated redneck drawl, "That ain't no Amerkin ayack-sent." She pretended to strum an air banjo, wailing a country song I was not familiar with, heaping on the hayseed drawl with a manure shovel.

It dawned on me why they thought we were Canadian.

Just as I still cannot tell an Australian accent from a New Zealand or Tasmanian, they think everyone in the US talks like the Dukes of Hazzard. Of course, after a month in the country, I realized that the only Americans on Australian TV were either NASCAR drivers or President George W. Bush.

I was walking past a group of guys, several beers into the evening, when I heard the word "fish," and I stopped to listen. I was still not fluent with Aussie nicknames, so when one of the men said he planned on using "mulies" to catch "pinkies." I had to ask for a translation. They were talking about fishing for pink snappers. "Mulies" were some sort of small baitfish. Perhaps mullets? They also suggested that "ocky" was good bait, too, and stayed on the hook longer. Octopus. I think they have nicknames for words like "it" and "the."

The bottom line was that the local fishing—which the owner of the campground, a lively little red-faced woman, declared "famous"—was concentrated in one spot where a sandy spit offered shorebound anglers access to deep water. The trouble was that it was across a large bay and accessible only by boat. For a small fee they ferried people across and left them there to fish. All day. "Bring a lunch and plenty of drinks," she said. "We leave at 7:00 a.m."

My wife insisted that I should go. She would sleep late, she said, sit in the sun, walk on the beach, read five or six novels, watch the emus that roam the West Coast of Australia like pigeons. She would feed the wallabies Wheat Thins and potato chips. Not a problem with her at all. And it was certainly reasonable to believe that she might already want a little time to herself after a couple of days in a very small camper with me. But I wasn't sure.

This seemed like the classic setup for a vacation/fishing trip debacle. I would come back to the camper at three in the afternoon only to discover that Lin had stepped on a poisonous ant, the flying doctors had amputated her foot, and she had been medivaced to Sydney, three thousand kilometers away, where she was having a foot transplant operation. And I wasn't there all day and couldn't be reached. I was fishing.

But it was not just the memory of my Beaver Island family outing faux pas, it was the tackle the Aussies were using. The fact was I had not met one person who had ever seen a fly rod, let alone used one in these waters. I just wasn't too enthused about being dropped off on a desert island with a bunch of guys wielding surf rods and casting bait halfway to Madagascar, the next nearest land mass. When we had planned this trip, somehow I had envisioned the only kind of saltwater fishing I had ever done: flats fishing in the Caribbean. I pictured vast sandy shallows and Indian Ocean bonefish. But I could see by the rods in the campground that I was on the wrong continent. And I had little confidence in blind casting small, feathered hooks into a very large ocean.

I ate my burger with fried egg on it, had a couple more beers, and slept in late the next morning with my wife.

For the next few days we drove and camped and enjoyed the vastness of the huge, mostly unpopulated Western Australia outback. Outside of the state's one large city, Perth, there are only half a million people living in about a million and a half square miles of territory. I didn't try to fish again—not that I wasn't thinking about it as we proceeded down the coast, the Indian Ocean off to our right calling to me. Mostly, I just enjoyed the peaceful emptiness of the open road between camping sites. Sometimes we would drive for an hour or more and see only one other vehicle passing the other way. Even by Alaskan standards this was fabulously wild and untrammeled country. We live in the little town of Anchor Point, two hundred miles from Anchorage; we have a post office, two stores, one bar, and one and a half gas stations. That seems like living in a veritable metropolis compared to Western Australia.

To get a sense of the distances, consider this. A couple days south of Broome we stopped where a sidetrack flared off to our left: eastward, inland. There was a sign that said Marble Bar 202kmo. That's two hundred two kilometers, or about one hundred twenty-five miles of absolutely nothing but red sand and kangaroos—at the end of which is a town where, according to the travel guides, temperatures in excess of one hundred degrees were once recorded for one hundred sixty consecutive days. And this is not Phoenix, with palm trees and ten million sprinklers misting green lawns and golf courses. This is not Palm Springs, with air-conditioned restaurants on every other corner and real estate agents on the remaining ones. This is a mining camp in the middle of something called the Great Sandy Desert. The *Great* Sandy Desert? Can you imagine what it takes to be singled out with a name like that on a continent that looks at first glance to be nothing but sandy desert?

We studied our maps and peered down that side road; it disappeared over a small rise dotted with spinifex grass and stunted umbrella bushes. I tried to imagine the town of Marble Bar out there at the end of it, and beyond that no other habitation or human developments for more than two thousand kilometers until the north-south highway that bisects the continent. That's a lot of wilderness.

I thought about the kid named Chris McCandless who had famously perished a few miles off a major highway in Alaska. His doomed spirit quest fostered a bestselling book and Hollywood movie, not to mention a cult of admirers (very few Alaskans among them) who find a person who wanders off into the woods and starves to death somehow romantic. Boy, would those people love Australia.

I looked at the road sign and then at my wife. The sun beat on the hood of the camper van and on the pavement and on the dusty red dirt of the two-hundred-kilometer long road to Marble Bar. She is a really good sport. She said, "It might be interesting." I thought about it.

We had two large jerry cans of drinking water and two cans of diesel fuel. We had four-wheel-drive and flares. There was even an emergency locator beacon in the glove box: apparently, whatever happened to us, the rental company planned on getting its camper back. We probably wouldn't die. On the other hand, the gorgeous blue Indian Ocean was a few kilometers to our west. Let's face it: Slowly roasting to death in the relentless heat of the outback seemed even less appealing than a relatively quick death by shark or crocodile. And in all that white space on the map there was not one blue line indicating a river, not one lake of any kind. From where we sat at that turnoff, the next fishable water was on the Great Barrier Reef, thousands of kilometers of empty desert to the east. I pulled back out onto the wrong side of the highway and kept driving south.

RULE NUMBER THREE: FISH WHEN THE LOCALS FISH

We drove to Cape Range National Park and I did catch a few small fish I could not identify in my snorkeler's guide to Australian reef fish. But the place I had the most hope for, the place where, according to the tourist information I had read, I had the best probability of actually combining a family vacation with a fishing trip, was Francois Peron National Park, halfway between Broome and Perth. All we had to do was survive the trip there, maybe a thousand kilometers down the coast highway.

How bad could it be? Australia's only a smorgasbord of myriad dangers—I mean, other than the well-documented stuff, such as crocodiles, sharks, killer jellyfish, poisonous octopi, and eight of the ten deadliest snakes on earth. Everywhere we went there were signs warning of crumbling cliffs and murderous tide surges, rogue waves and poisonous everything. If I had seen a sign warning of man-eating butterflies or venomous dairy cows, I would have believed it in a minute. I had fished alongside the huge brown bears of Katmai for decades. They seemed downright cuddly compared to the animals in this country. And then there were the larger natural phenomena. After being there a month, my impression was that, at any given moment, there was either a drought or a flood or a cyclone or a massive, raging brush fire killing people somewhere in this brutal land.

That said, there is probably nothing in Australia more dangerous than its roads—which may seem unlikely given the paucity of drivers out there in the Outback, the fact that there are no towns for hundreds of kilometers, no intersections for hours, and no two-legged pedestrians, except for the emus, which have bird brains enough to flap their useless wings and run like hell as you approach. There are, however, road trains.

Because there are almost no railroad lines in this vast region, all the resources produced or extracted here—all the cattle and sheep, all the iron ore, gold, and other minerals—have to go to the coastal seaports by truck. Since there are also very, very few cars on the road except for the odd terrified Alaskan tourist or two, the truckers are permitted to tow an apparently limitless number of trailers behind their rigs. They are also, apparently, permitted to ignore all international standards of driving safety and the Geneva Convention as well. The result is, as the name suggests, speeding train-length trucks laden with everything from bananas and mangoes to coal, gypsum, and live four-legged animals. You think 18-wheelers are scary when they pass you? Try 46-wheelers in a country where speed limits are considered suggestions.

Then again, if you were towing three huge trailers of perishable goods in hundred-degree heat, driving what is basically a diesel locomotive over hundreds of kilometers of mostly empty roads, trying to make a living, how would you drive? If your answer is, "Like a goddamn maniac!" you're absolutely right. One typically sardonic Aussie told me that if a trucker kills more than three tourists in a calendar year he could lose his job. In fact, mostly what road trains do kill are animals. Lots of them.

Everywhere we drove in Western Australia, the shoulders of the roads were littered with dead animals. Because kangaroos, wallabies, and livestock of every variety swarm across the country roads like mice at night, the camper rental agency warned us not to drive after dark—at all. We found out what they meant one evening when we lingered on the dunes of Cape Range National Park watching a flaming red Indian Ocean sunset and found ourselves driving back to camp in near darkness. We counted more than thirty black-footed wallabies crossing the road in less than ten kilometers.

Road train drivers, on the other hand, love to drive at night. With fewer tourists in their way, they can really get up some speed. As I said, the roads there are strewn with kangaroo carcasses, dead cows, pigs, goats, and sheep, and even a boa constrictor or two. To avoid damage to the front ends of the trucks caused by the numerous animals they flatten, the enormous rigs have heavy, curved steel pipes called roo bars welded across their grillwork. Every time I saw one roar up behind us in our side view mirrors, I couldn't help thinking that those gleaming steel bumper pipes could also be called tourist bars.

But, in truth, Australians love tourists. As if to compensate for their deadly wildlife, inhospitable terrain, and homicidal truck drivers, Australians in general are absurdly friendly. Everywhere we went we merely uttered one sentence and someone would say, "Is that a North American accent?" Immediately the camp chairs came out, along with maps and journey notes, recommendations on camper parks and snorkeling sites, jokes and stories about snakes and crocodiles and unfortunate American tourists, a wine bottle or two. And then came the questions about Alaska. How did we stand the cold? Was there really endless darkness? And my personal favorite: "Aren't there a lot of dangerous animals?"

In the big camper parks near the towns of Port Hedland and Exmouth and Dampier, people gathered around the public barbecue grills and there was often some guy in a floppy hat strumming a guitar, singing pithy Outback folk songs (give me snakes any day). The camaraderie was thick and genuine: lots of guys drinking beer, cleaning fish, laughing; lots of women drinking chardonnay, hanging laundry on the community clotheslines, chatting. We would move in and set up camp, and the Aussie welcome wagon would show up before we had the cork out of a shiraz. But even in the most remote settings, the Australian penchant for company was startling, and, we came to learn, ultimately delightful.

About halfway to Perth, we took the long detour up into a peninsula that contained the Francois Peron National Park and my best hopes for a fishing adventure. To get to the beach we had to let most of the air out of our tires and drive—often in four-wheel low, low gear—for hours across deep sand and desolate, potholed clay pans. At the end of this, however, was not just more of the predictably gorgeous Indian Ocean, but the Ningaloo Reef, Australia's lesser-known barrier reef on its western coast. It is a destination worth crawling on your hands and knees to reach. There might even be fly fishing there.

In the guidebooks, the park was described as "undeveloped." I told my wife that meant that if we got lost it might be a few days before the rangers find whatever the buzzards had left of our bodies. Really it meant there were outhouses in designated camping areas, but there was no fresh water or any other amenities.

Forty kilometers of sand roads and no fresh water also meant there were no crowds. Actually, when we arrived there was no one there. Period. The rough ride in requires four-wheel-drive vehicles with high clearance and the spartan facilities are not everyone's cup of yellow beer. So when we finally got to the coast we were pleased to find that the camping area in the dunes overlooking the ocean was completely uninhabited. There were six or eight good-looking flat places to park. We picked one near the far end of the sand track where it petered out into impassible rock and scrub. We were alone except for the wallabies and lizards.

"Oh my God," one or both of us said. A family of porpoises rolled into the lagoon as a small flock of gray and pink parrots drifted by overhead. "We have this place to ourselves?"

We settled in, gloating over our incredible luck. Miles and miles of beach and not another soul in sight. Delightfully named "splendid fairywrens" fidgeted from twig to twig in the umbrella bushes, wagging their erect blue tails behind them as we cracked open the vodka bottle and sliced a lemon and ensconced ourselves in canvas lawn chairs. The reef was only two hundred yards offshore. Three adult dolphins and one baby were still swimming in the protected crystal clear shallows of what we had already come to think of as "our" bay. Talk about once in a lifetime.

I sat back in my chair with the late afternoon sun low in the west over the horizon. I studied the blue lagoon at our doorstep, planning where I would start fishing in the morning, imagining the exotic game fish I would catch. I mean, what do porpoises eat?

My wife took a seat beside me, smiling happily, thinking about whatever people who do not fish think about when they get near water. I have no idea.

With more than a little pride in our own intrepidness, we toasted each other and our good luck in finding such a paradise, and saluted Australia, a modern developed nation that still had seaside campgrounds with empty sites available. And with the first sip of our drinks still cool on our smug little lips we heard the shifting of gears, the strain of an engine pulling a vehicle through the sand, coming our way. Other fishermen, I thought.

They picked the spot next to us, thirty feet away. I'm not making this up. There was, seriously, at least a half-mile of vehicle-accessible camping area there, all of it empty. But they wanted to be next to us. "They" turned out to be Dave Marshal and his wife Susan, their daughters Maya (age two) and Shaan (five) and a nursing infant named Baby Jack. Dave and Susan were schoolteachers, and were on holiday from the town of Albany, southeast of Perth, almost a thousand kilometers away. If you'd like to know anything more about them, anything at all, I can tell you, because for the next week we were more or less one big family. And it was the best week of the whole trip.

My wife and I enjoyed the little girls immensely. Like every adult Australian we had met, the children seemed intent on moving in with us too. Shaan, the older one, showed us the shells and crab claws she had collected on the beach. Two-year-old Maya told us convoluted stories in her impenetrable Aussie baby talk, which we pretended to understand. They woke up each morning screaming with laughter and spent much of the day running barefoot across jagged limestone ridges that made me wince and whimper. They fell and cut themselves and laughed. They leapt into the cold winter water and laughed. We decided that they were either going to be movie stars or road train drivers.

Their father, Dave, was smart and funny and a skilled snorkeler who went out each day in a wet suit to spear fresh fish for the grill. This reminded me of Rule Number Two: Fish How the Locals Fish. Meaning a fly rod was not the way to catch the fish on the Ningaloo Reef, a spear gun was. But there was nothing I could do about that. Dave gave us an estuary cod that had flesh every bit as flaky and oily and sweet as our North Pacific grey cod at home in Alaska. A day or two later he speared a fish called a coral trout that had a hot orange head with florescent blue spots and was even more prized as a food fish. We cooked them both on the barbecue grill. Dave showed us how to pry oysters off the rocks using a tire iron and a hammer—something else you can't do with a fly rod. I fished every morning, early, before my wife or the family next door awoke, but the whole week, I caught only a handful of tiny reef fish and surf perch of some kind.

One morning I waded to the edge of the reef and stood on the brutally pointed limestone rocks casting into the clear sea. Our camper and Dave and Susan's truck and tent were the only signs of humans. The sun was coming up over the huge desert to the east of us and then a wallaby hopped out of the scrub onto the beach and stopped to look at me, its shadow stretched all the way to the water's edge. Flycatchers twittered in the bushes. An Australian raven laughed: Haw, haw, hawwwww. I was casting into the Indian Ocean on a beach out of a travel brochure, all by myself. I was not catching anything, true. But whose fault was that?

The wallaby bounded off and I started walking back to camp, thinking about coffee and whatever fresh fruit we had left. We were almost out of everything, fresh water being the most critical item in very short supply. We needed showers. We would have to leave this paradise and this wonderful adopted family the next morning and make the long drive across the sandy desert back to the main road. I didn't want it to end. I also wanted to catch one good fish before we left this beautiful place.

I was stumbling over the jagged reef rocks, when, out of the corner of my eye, I caught a movement in the water to my left. I spun and saw the unmistakable torpedo shadow of a predator fish cruising the wave edge less than forty feet away. An easy cast. For someone who was vigilant and prepared. For someone else.

As I stumbled across the rocks, my fly had flopped around the rod tip and tangled. The fish, whatever it was—something about the size of a permit or a very large bonefish—continued along the edge of the reef, hunting. I stood and watched helplessly as the first good shot at a fish I had been offered in nearly a thousand kilometers of Australian coastline vanished. It was one of those moments every fisherman has when he wonders what golf or bridge or flower arranging might be like for hobbies.

That afternoon, new campers joined us on the bay: a group of four middle-aged folks with several tents, propane refrigerators, and a trailer full of fresh water barrels that indicated they planned on being there a while. They set up camp on the other side of us. After dinner, as my wife and I sat watching what would be our last sunset at this beautiful lagoon, I was interested to see the new people traipsing down to the water with fishing rods in hand. Soon there was the unmistakable whooping sound of an angler with a fish on the line. It turns out that each evening, when the sun is low in the west, schools of tailor fish come into the lagoon to feed a short cast's distance from the beach. Would they take a fly? Nobody there knew. They had never tried it. And neither would I. Our drinking water was almost gone. We left in the morning.

POSTSCRIPT

Earlier in the month, and several hundred kilometers back, we took a side trip one morning that I haven't mentioned. We were on our way south after a couple days at Cape Range, when, not too far from the town of Carnarvon, on the ocean side of the road we came across a sign that said Blowholes. It was early in the day, so I—with no fishing motives in mind and being an uncommonly good sport about it—drove down to the shore to gape at the natural phenomenon. The eponymous blowholes were everything they were advertised in our travel guide books: a kind of saltwater, mini Old Faithful. The shore was a huge rocky monolith for several hundred yards, deeply undercut by the wave action. On each incoming roller, water blasted out of a cluster of holes in the rock at our feet and spumed fifty feet in the air. We oohed and aahed and pointed appropriately and took photos and got sprayed. It was a very touristy thing to do, and nothing about the open ocean waves or the rocky shore suggested rigging up a fly rod. It was a pleasantly unconflicted moment.

But as we turned the camper around to depart, I noticed a large bay a short distance down the coast from the blowholes. There was a sandy beach, and people were camping in tents and shacks made of corrugated metal and canvas tarps. The bay was protected from the open ocean swells by a huge rock formation blocking the mouth. Everything about the place looked to me like a perfect sandy bonefish flat. I stared at this appealing water for a long time, the fisherman's instincts rising in my gut. But there were miles to go yet, and so many more places to fish still ahead of us. We drove on.

After our lovely—though fishless—week on the beach in Francois Peron park, we spent a few far-more-civilized days in a well-kept camper park in the town of Kalbarri. In keeping with my new resolution to forget about fishing, I was sitting in a lovely coffee shop having one of those cups of coffee with a European sounding name and a massive price tag when I noticed a stack of magazines lying nearby. I figured this must be how people who do not fish pass the time on vacations: drinking overpriced coffee and reading other people's magazines. I picked up something called *The Western Australian Fishing Magazine*. Yes. And, yes again. There was an article about a bonefish hotspot at—you already guessed it—the Blowholes, ten days and maybe five hundred kilometers behind us. Apparently anglers drove all the way from Perth to fish there. The magazine also mentioned what a nice camping spot it was for a family holiday.

Chapter 16

The Trevally Ripped Our Flesh!

Four thousand miles from our homes in Alaska, my three traveling companions and I—all first-timers to Christmas Island—gawked out the windows of our Air Pacific 737 as it descended toward the impressively named but decidedly rustic Cassidy International Airport. Below us, miles of fishy-looking shallows stretched to the horizon as the plane came in over the island's one hundred and fifty square mile lagoon, a protected expanse of white sand flats: feeding grounds for bonefish, milkfish, three species of trevally, and a host of other inshore fish just begging for someone to throw a fly at them.

Christmas Island (Kiritimati in the local language) is one of the thirty-three atolls that make up the Republic of Kiribati, a country with the lowest overall elevations of any land on earth, and the nation predicted to be the first to disappear when sea levels rise another couple feet. Situated almost smack on both the equator and the International Date Line, Christmas Island lies eleven hundred miles of open ocean south of Hawaii. As famous as the sport fishing has become there, the big jets do not provide service to the remote mid-Pacific speck for the convenience of fly fishers, or even for the five thousand local inhabitants; it is a refueling stop for flights from Honolulu to Fiji. Near the airport are the remnants of a gigantic World War II runway complex built by American armed forces to prevent the Japanese military from occupying and using the island for their own refueling.

Customs and security checks behind us, Bob, Will, Debra, and I rode in the bed of an old Chevy pickup past clusters of small concrete block houses and thatch-roofed huts that made up several small roadside villages. Along the road, blooming plumeria trees glowed radiantly white; pigs and chickens loitered in the shade of coconut palms; skinny yellow dogs ran to meet impeccably neat children returning home from school. Just outside Banana Village, we turned off onto a two-track through the saltbushes and down to the beach and the lodge, ominously named A Shark's Place. We arrived just in time for cocktails and fresh *hamachi*—yellowtail tuna sashimi.

Missing, however, were the two other Alaskans in our group who had been at the lodge for a week before us, Matt and Dave. They had not returned from a day of blue water fishing, and the lodge staff was as concerned as we were by the time the flaming evening sun slid behind the breadfruit trees. When Matt and Dave finally staggered in, an hour after dark, their account of a dead outboard, the satellite phone they'd left on shore, and the two-way radio their guide had also forgotten to take onboard, sounded like a perfect example of chaos theory. Given the island's isolation (Tarawa, the country's capital, is on another island, more than two thousand miles away), they could have drifted halfway to Papua New Guinea before the closest Coast Guard base (Honolulu) mounted a search wide enough to locate them. Luckily a local fishing boat saw them waving madly, and towed them in.

Being Alaskans, none of us had felt actual warm sunshine on our pasty white skin since August of last year. So we set out for the flats the next morning dressed in tropical sunproof hoodies and neck gaiters, sun gloves and billowing nylon wading pants. Climbing into the forty-foot plywood outrigger canoe with our guides, we looked like lost beduins, or maybe bandits intent on robbing a train with fly rods.

The big boat was used only for navigating the labyrinthine channels of the huge lagoon. All the fishing at Christmas Island is done on foot, wading the firm sandy bottom, a flats fisherman's dream. The bonefish were plentiful, if not huge, but very hard to see with scudding clouds obscuring the light off and on all day. At times all we could do was stop wading and wait for the sun to break through again. More than once, when the light went back on, we discovered bonefish so close that casting to them was nearly impossible with the heavy section of the line still in the rod guides, and only the leader and six feet of the taper in the air. Still, we caught enough bones to keep it interesting, and had the pleasure of blundering onto other flats species, including queenfish, golden trevally, and a couple small bluefin trevally.

The critter that really sparked my interest, though, was the brilliant orange-and-brown-patterned triggerfish. Triggers—which can grow to twenty pounds—are much easier to see than bones, of course, and are often found tailing in the coral around the deep holes they excavate while foraging. They will attack a small and very slow-moving fly—if you can set it in front of them without hanging up in the coral. Once you hook one, your troubles are just beginning: their rock-crunching teeth can cut through heavy stainless steel hooks like they're made of dental floss. And once hooked, a trigger's first exuberant run often ends with a dive into a hole or small cave, parting the tippet on the razor sharp coral edges. Still, I would happily spend a week fishing for nothing but triggers. At least I can see them without a guide—even on a cloudy day.

In spite of the huge numbers of bonefish cruising the endless flats, the fishing remained challenging—partly because the clouds only thickened over the next two days, but also because the bones were as finicky as housecats at times, forcing us to go to smaller and sparser flies for more consistent hookups. But that's what makes them such a great game fish; that and the ability of even a fifteen-incher to put a bend in an 8-weight saltwater rod, a rod stiff enough to launch a similar-sized trout into the trees behind you. It's also nice to fish someplace where the flats are virtually limitless, knowing you'll never wade the same water twice during your stay.

The weather deteriorated a little more each day. The flatness of the island allows a mostly unobstructed view in all four compass directions, and by mid week, black skies smothered the horizon on every side. Of course, the guides—all locals with years of experience walking these flats—can probably spot bonefish blindfolded in the middle of a moonless night. But spending the day blind casting to the guide's instructions, while it will certainly put fish in your hands—"Cast! Thirty feet! Ten o'clock! Ok, strip strip!"—is not exactly what we traveled half the globe to do. So, on the darkest morning, we took a very long drive to the open ocean side of the island and a stretch of beach called the Korean Wreck—named after a ship that went aground there in the 1970s. There a small reef parallels the white sandy beach just a hundred yards offshore, and the shallow little lagoon between the breakers and the beach is paved with moss-covered rocks, which attract milkfish.

By the time we waded into the lagoon, the rain was coming down in sheets. But, even so, spotting milkfish was easy. We could see hundreds of tails jutting through the surface as big schools of them grazed on the mossy bottom. Stalking them was easy; they are not nearly as spooky as bones. Casting to them was easy; the wind was offshore and mostly blocked by the low sand dunes and scrub brush. So how hard could it be to catch one? Well, one of the basic tenets of fly fishing is that the less willing to take a fly a fish is, the worthier it is to fish for. Milkfish—who eat nothing but vegetation—make permit look like the fish you'd stock a pond with for a children's fishing derby.

I cast one of the preferred milkfish patterns—a bit of green yarn or dubbing bound to a saltwater hook—right into the middle of the tailing fish thirty or forty times before lunch, only to have it ignored. Think about it: the milkfish are simply munching on algae and other vegetable detritus broken up by the waves. Your fly, even when dropped right in front of them, is just another speck of green junk—one among thousands, if not millions of others just like it. Fishing for them is like casting to Henry's Fork rainbows in the midst of a blanket baetis hatch. The odds of a fish eating your fly are probably the same—incalculably awful.

Yes, the milks do get big (upwards of thirty pounds). And yes, they do put up a tremendous fight (I'm told). But by that logic, you might as well cast that grassy-looking fly into a herd of cows and hope one of them sucks it up with a mouthful of alfalfa. (I'll bet if you strip-strike a hook into the lip of a full grown Holstein, you'll need more than an 8-weight to get it to the net.)

Under the careful tutelage of Moana—the senior guide and basically the godfather of fly fishing on Christmas Island—four of us cast all day in mostly pouring rain to school after school of milks and never touched one. Instead we all caught bonefish on the little grass flies—mostly when we were stripping the line in to cast again. One of our Alaskan friends caught a milkfish the week before. So, it is possible. But casting a fly and letting it lie still enough to replicate a piece of spinach is not my idea of fascinating fishing.

In fact, the memorable part of the day was finding out that the lightweight nylon windbreaker I'd brought along—in spite of hearing nothing but how unbearably hot Christmas Island is—had lost its waterproofing. I was soaked to the skin as we set out on the nearly two-hour truck ride back to the lodge. Since the roads are largely just paths between palm trees and scrubby thickets, and there was no sign of human habitation anywhere outside of the towns, our driver, Michael, kept the accelerator to the floor at all times except when a particularly deep-looking rain-filled pothole loomed before us. Which meant that we hurtled homeward at about fifty miles an hour, the wind rushing down my neck and through my waterlogged clothes. Without a very long and warm hug from Will's wife, Debra, I would have become one of the few persons known to have suffered hypothermia at sea level on the equator.

If milkfish fishing is a little too sophisticated for me, then chumming for trevally is crude enough to suit me perfectly—and exactly what the doctor ordered for another cloudy day. Even I must admit that tossing a bucketful of chopped up baitfish off the edge of a pancake flat and then casting a fly into the maelstrom of frenzied predators it draws is about as classy as baiting bears with old donuts (very popular in Alaska). But it was not a good day for bonefish, so pragmatism prevailed. Setting aside all pretenses of lofty principals, we waded to the edge of the flat, 12-weight rods in hand. Ethical concerns vanished when the surface of the channel exploded with rampaging GTs swarming up the blood scent trail.

Giant trevally. What a great name. I mean, would anybody travel thousands of miles to chum up *diminutive trevally*? Or *pygmy trevally*? No way. When we first started planning this trip, I asked a friend who had fished for GTs before what he could tell me about them. His exact words were: "Nothing can prepare you for their savagery." I thought that sounded a little hyperbolic (the guy *is* a writer). I was wrong. The four of us caught fifteen or twenty fish that day and every one of them took us far into the backing. At one point, Will lifted a foot-long queenfish to the surface foul-hooked in the tail. As he lowered the rod to strip line in, the squirming fish dove back under the surface. Big mistake. Will's rod bent double under the weight of the trevally that inhaled the hapless little fish. In minutes, the GT peeled two hundred yards of backing off his reel and cut him off on coral somewhere on the far side of the channel; he lost his whole fly line. Among the eight anglers in camp that week, we lost five fly lines entirely, cut three more lines in half, and broke two 12-weight rods. By the end of the week, various members of our group were wearing back braces, thumb splints, and/or cervical collars. On a map of Christmas Island you will see a place on the outside shore labeled Bay of Wrecks. It could have been named for us.

As GTs go—giant trevally can grow to more than a hundred pounds—the ones we caught that day were fairly small, mostly in the ten- to twenty-pound range. That's really just as well. After the initial thrill of realizing you've set your hook into a fish that even sharks avoid, the battle with a heavy GT becomes something like a weight-lifting competition: lots of grunting and not much action. My friend Bob landed one that weighed forty pounds or more, and took nearly half an hour to come to hand. At one point, Will and Bob and I had three GTs on at once, fish going in three directions, us slipping and tripping trying to stay untangled, Deb, madly attempting to capture the hilarity on film. I have to say that the preposterousness of the whole thing—three grown men, splashing around up to our hips in the water, hooting and laughing, rods bent double—was a refreshing reminder of what fishing meant to us all when we first tried it so many years ago, back when the fish on the ends of our lines might have been bluegills or bullheads or chubs: in a word, *fun*.

Our last day on the island, the sun shone brightly. It was going to be a great day for bonefish. But, for our last hurrah, Bob and I chose to hang up the fly rods and go exploring the deep blue sea. Trolling from the back of the huge outrigger canoe with lightweight spinning rods and lures the size of the bonefish we'd been catching produced some of the best memories of the whole trip.

Bob hooked up first, and brought a nice yellowfin tuna almost to the boat. Then we found out why our lodge is named A Shark's Place; only the head of the tuna came up. The next hookup (also Bob) was a big wahoo that put up a hell of a fight—and made some great ceviche later that evening. And then we both hooked up in a double that turned out to be two heavy yellowfins. Incredibly, both fish were hooked badly. Bob's was foul-hooked near the pectoral fin, and my fish had the tail hook of the big Rapalla plug in its mouth, but the front hook snagged in its gill plate. Anyone who has hooked a large fish somewhere aft of its mouth knows that the fish has only to tilt its pectorals and the harder you pull the more it planes away from you. With two big tuna planing in enormous circles under the boat and crossing our lines over and over again, it took us an hour and a half to get them both in.

If not for the aching muscles, joints, bones, and titanium hardware Bob and I both have bolted to our spines, I'm sure it would have been quite comical. Let's just say we've never paid more for fresh *hamachi* in our lives.

Christmas Island has everything a fisherman of any level of sophistication could desire. For serious fly fishers, the bonefish can be satisfyingly difficult at times, the milkfish delightfully impossible. For a guy with a sense of humor and lots of extra tackle, a bucket of chopped-up bait will bring in all the giant trevally and comic relief you can stand. And for knuckle-dragging troglodytes, like, say, me for example, you can take 800 mg of Ibuprofen, cinch on your back brace, and find out what a fifty-pound tuna feels like on the end of a light spinning rod. But remember: the electricity does not run all night. So don't bother bringing your heating pad.

Chapter 17

Slamming Cuba

SWORN ENEMIES

I was just a kid when Nikita Khrushchev, leader of the fearsome Soviet Empire, America's sworn enemy, installed a bristling thicket of Soviet nuclear missiles on his pal Fidel's island ninety miles south of Florida in October of 1962. It looked like Khrushchev really did intend to bury us, as he had promised. Or, more accurately, cremate us in an atomic firestorm.

I was fourteen years old. I didn't want to be buried or cremated anytime soon. Still don't.

Although our country called his bluff, and the warheads were shipped back to Russia, Cuba remained a vaguely ominous presence to me for the next half a century—sort of like living down the road from a guy who sits on his porch cleaning his rifle every time you drive by. So early this year (2015), when my longtime fishing pal, photographer, and writer Will Rice called to ask if I wanted to go fish that once forbidden island, I might have hesitated a little. A lot, actually.

I mean, the Iron Curtain may be folded up and packed in mothballs now, but Russia and Cuba are still pretty chummy. And the guy in the big chair in the Kremlin today is clearly as least as crazy as Khrushchev ever was.

Will said, "Listen, about forty miles off the south coast of Cuba there's a place called Cayo Largo, an island at the heart of more than four hundred square miles of carefully managed bonefish and tarpon preserve. A flats fishing paradise." He let me take the bait, then set the hook: "They've caught five hundred permit there in the last five years."

That did it. Five hundred permit. Are you kidding me? Nuclear annihilation? Ha. I laugh at nuclear annihilation. To get odds like that for a permit, I'd march into North Korea and kiss Kim Jong Un on the lips.

Permit! I've been trying to get one of those willful, picky, uncooperative bastards to eat a fly since 1996. I have cast to them in Ascension Bay, up and down the barrier reef off Belize, on Abaco Island, the Cayman Islands, and on the southern Yucatán Peninsula. Maybe a couple other places I've thankfully forgotten. And each time one of them came up behind the fly I'd offered, it opened its mouth to bite and then suddenly turned away. You've heard of a gaggle of geese and a murder of crows? A group of *Trachinotus falcatus* is called a "refusal" of permits. Or it should be.

In 2011, after fifteen permitless years, I nearly quit flats fishing altogether. How much humiliation does a man need to take? In the last five years, the only trip I agreed to was Christmas Island, and only because there are no permit in that part of the Pacific. So, why would I possibly, after all those nerve-wracking failures, agree to go to Cuba and face my finny nemeses once more? Why?

The Avalon Fly. That's why.

I'm one of those guys who believes there exists one magical fly pattern that will not merely catch whatever species of fish I am currently pursuing, but will haul them in like a pollock seiner. Every time I clamp a hook in a vise, I'm convinced I am about to tie such a fly. So the rumor of a whole new, and putatively deadly, permit fly pattern obliterated fifty years of Cold War paranoia like a direct hit from an MRBM.

The Avalon Fly was designed by Cayo Largo lodge manager Mauro Ginevri and his super permit guide, William Guanche, to imitate the local, pale-colored shrimp that are a major item on the Cuban permit's menu. As of the day Will and I arrived on Cayo Largo, the fly had landed 566 permit since its inception in 2009. It has also caught innumerable bonefish, snook, and even tarpon, not to mention untargeted species: mutton snappers, jacks, barracuda. Basically, anything that eats shrimp is a sucker for this fly.

Still, the question was: What if—even armed with a box full of the secret weapon Avalon flies—the permit of Cuba flummoxed me like they had everywhere else I had fished for them? Where was I supposed to go next?

OUT OF BALANCE

One of the welcome surprises on Cayo Largo is the accommodations. Avalon Cuban Fishing Centers puts their anglers up at the Sol Club Cayo Largo, an "all inclusive" extravaganza of a place right out of the Fantasy Island TV show. Hundreds of rooms, a spectacular white sand beach, four restaurants, numerous fully stocked bars (all drinks included in the price!), swimming pools, tennis courts, even a *bocce* court for your inner Italian. You name it. In short, everything needed for whatever the hell it is that people who don't fish do while on vacation. Personally, I think sitting on the beach at Cayo Largo all day and not fishing would be like staying up all night in Vegas bowling.

The rooms—which come with fastidious maids—are designed for normal, comfort-seeking civilized people, not obsessed permit fishermen, and only served to show me what knuckle-dragging cretins Will and I have been all our fishing lives. In Belize, we stayed in a shack on stilts on a mud and mangrove island that is submerged under an inch of water on full moon tides. On Christmas Island, our rooms were cinder block bunkers. In the Yucatán, lizards prowled the thatched roofs of our palapas and cockroaches tap-danced under the beds. All of which was fine. We were there to fish.

Having lived in Alaska for more than thirty years, most of my local fishing trips mean sleeping bags in wind-wracked tents with huge bears (and mosquitos not much smaller) prowling outside them. Now, in my dotage, I could happily get accustomed to fishing out of immaculate rooms with tiled floors and mini bars full of complimentary Havana Club rum and Cristal beers. With age comes wisdom. And decadence.

After checking in, I was out on the balcony changing a fly line on a reel, nervously anticipating our first day of fishing the next morning. Will was in the hotel room spreading camera gear and fishing tackle across his bed.

When a friendly guy from the balcony next to ours called out in vaguely Scandinavian-inflected English, "You are fly fishing?" I admitted I was. He grinned and said, "Then you'll want to see this." He fetched his camera and handed it over the railing separating us.

On the digital screen, the man—his name was Eiskert and he was Norwegian—stood on the deck of a flats boat gripping a permit the size of a truck tire.

"Holy shit!" I yelped. "Will, get out here and look at the size of this fucker!"

Eiskert informed us that he had caught it only the day before, his last day of fishing there at Cayo Largo that week. Yes, it was permit number 566 caught on the Avalon Fly. His guide was the amazing William, who later told us that Eiskert's permit was, in fact, the largest one he had ever seen in his fourteen years guiding there. They estimated it at thirty pounds.

Eiskert is a very serious angler. Tattooed in blue ink on his left forearm are line drawings of a bonefish, a tarpon, a permit, and a snook, and the words *Super Grand Slam, Cuba, 2011.* He also showed us the tattoo of a shark on his right calf. It said, *Greenland Shark, 2001, 1100 kg* (that's about twenty-three hundred pounds).

It was the second largest fish of any kind ever taken on sport fishing tackle. I have a feeling Eiskert fishes like a Norseman on a pillaging run up the coast of old Normandy. I picture him on the casting deck wearing a horned helmet, fly rod in one hand, double-edged broadax in the other.

That first night on the island, I had a hard time falling asleep—in spite of several rum drinks and the exhaustion of traveling over five thousand miles from Alaska, the trip taking more hours than I care to think about. Thoughts of Eiskert's fishing triumphs flashed through my brain, but it was not a shark the size of a small submarine that haunted me. It was the photo of our strapping Norwegian neighbor straining to hold that thirty-pound slab of permit out for the camera.

I flopped around on the bed in the warm Cuban air, the AC doing the best it could but not really geared to cool thick-blooded Alaskans. I was thankful for the ceiling fan, but it was out of balance and emitted a repetitive, two-syllable, guttural sound on each grinding revolution. All night long I heard it saying, "permit, permit, permit, permit, permit . . ."

THERE WILL BE MUD

The first day of fishing, I caught the first tarpon of my life and also my first snook—a species I'd never even seen before.

I hooked the snook up against a log-strewn bank and managed to keep it out of the sticks long enough to get it to the boat. The tarpon showed up while poling the same shoreline, and ate the same fly the snook fell for—a black and purple "tarpon toad" pattern. We also sight-fished to tailing bones in ankle-deep water in a mangrove maze, similarly struggling, with mixed success, to keep hooked fish out of the barnacle-studded roots

It was a great day, sunny and nearly windless, and having landed a bonefish, a tarpon, and a snook, we joked that I'd caught a quasi-grand slam. Of, course, the permit is the fish that makes or breaks a true slam, and I'd blown every cast to them that day. No surprise there. I'd been doing that for two decades. But the week was just starting.

Having caught two new species, I slept soundly that night, although through my dreams I heard that ceiling fan muttering its mantra. If I had landed a marlin, a tuna, and a white whale that day, I'd still have wanted a permit. Compared to me, Melville's Ahab was a poster child for mental health.

On the second morning, the light and the wind weren't right for the open-ocean permit flats, so we spent some time fishing a channel for rolling tarpon, and Will caught a nice one that jumped all over the sky before coming in. But after lunch it was time to go out to the muds.

Racing across mile upon mile of water as clear as white rum, we started to see huge, nearly opaque ovals of cloudy blue-gray soup on the surface in the distance. They looked like nothing more than cloud shadows at first. But as we approached one, William cut the engine and we rocked to a halt; I could see that we were near the edge of maybe five acres of muddied water.

It was my turn on deck. William climbed the poling platform and poled the boat to within a hundred yards of an enormous mud cloud created by stingrays and hundreds, maybe thousands, of bonefish rooting in the soft bottom for clams and sea worms. The mud they stir up drifts downwind, and along the direction of the tide and ocean currents. The whole area swirls with uncountable bonefish, snappers, jacks, needlefish, boxfish, and every other imaginable kind of inshore species congregating in these muds to feed on the shrimp and baitfish dislodged by the bottom-feeders. Sharks and barracuda move in to prey on anything smaller than themselves. The result is a maelstrom of feeding fish. And, most importantly, it includes permit. Lots of them.

If you cast just about any fly into the mud cloud itself, you will almost certainly hook something—usually a bonefish, because they are probably the most numerous species in the frenzied feeding zone, and among the fastest and first to get to the fly. But blind casting is like blind dating. I mean, yes, you'll catch lots of fish, but it is about as enjoyable as having dinner with a strange woman who wants to talk about her food allergies.

William moved us along the perimeter of the huge mud keeping the boat far enough away to see fish darting out into the clear water in pursuit of escaping bait. Within minutes, he said, "Permit. Eleven o'clock, thirty meters. Wait!" He jammed the pole into the bottom to turn the boat, and I peered into the sunny glare, not seeing anything but water. "Where?" I said. "I can't see them." And then I could.

Maybe fifty feet out off the port beam, there was a small "refusal" of permit unmistakably flashing gold highlights off their sickle fins and scissor-like tails as they zigzagged through some kind of panicked bait.

"Cast," William said, "Twenty meters."

For once, the gods of permit fishing smiled. The fly landed just short of the fish. I stripped two, maybe three times, and saw the permit—now five or six of them, at least—turn and race after the fly. I kept stripping, the fish following behind it toward the boat. Miraculously, the fly was not ambushed by a snapper, a jack, or even a pesky bonefish. (On Cayo Largo the bonefish are so big and fat they make Christmas Island and Ascension Bay bones look like lawn darts. Yet they are also so plentiful that five-pounders stealing your fly out from under the noses of permit actually seem like a nuisance.) Two strips more, and the fastest or hungriest of the permit pounced. The line went tight, and started flying off the screaming reel. My two-decade slump ended fifteen minutes later when Will took a photo of Cayo Largo permit number 567 caught on the Avalon Fly.

I figure I'll stop grinning in another month or so.

It was two-thirty in the afternoon. What was I supposed to do with the rest of the day? With the rest of my life? Besting your nemesis has its downside.

"Still enough time for a grand slam," William said. "Let's go find some tarpon." He started the Yamaha four-stroke.

A grand slam. Another reason to live. Thank God.

OH BABY, OH BABY!

One of the other perks of fishing Cayo Largo is the fabulous possibility of a grand slam—which is not too hard, once you've caught a permit. Of course, that's like saying "it's easy being wealthy: all you have to do is have lots of money." But, seriously, look at the statistics: Last year (2014) Cayo Largo had sixty-four grand slams, and twenty-two super grand slams (permit, bonefish, tarpon, and snook).

The Avalon Fly, the boundless flats, and the finely-honed guiding services there give anglers more really promising shots at permit than anywhere on earth. Bonefish are prolific. And though giant tarpon are mostly available only in late spring and early summer, the resident year-round five- to twenty-pound toddlers ensure the probability of a grand slam—again, once you've caught a permit. All that really remains is to find a baby tarpon, and the guides are practically on a first name basis with them.

With two hours of fishing time left on the clock, William roared inland from the ocean flats and plowed to a stop in a mangrove jungle lagoon. Slowly poling along the edges of the trees, he soon spotted tarpon lurking under overhanging branches. Nothing to it, right? This was going to be easy.

Not.

Two hours later, and more botched casts than I care to enumerate, I was still thrashing the water. I put the big size two-ought fly into the trees again and again. I slammed it on top of the fish and spooked them. I wrapped the line around the tip of the rod. I hit myself in the back of the head. There is almost no example of bad casting I did not demonstrate that afternoon, trying to complete the grand slam.

William's patience ran thin. I could hear exasperation in his voice. But he still continued to encourage me. "Just cast it straight in there between those two trees and under that log. See them in there? You can do it."

Yes, I saw the fish parked behind a log under a wall of towering mangroves. But actually I could *not* do it. I could cast it across the log and get snagged. I could launch it into the mangrove branches above. That I could do. And I did.

William smiled as he poled us in close enough to extract the fly from the foliage. "It's ok. We'll keep looking."

I cast into more trees. I cast into thick mats of surface weeds. I cast into everything but the tarpon we kept seeing loitering in groups under the overhanging trees like commuters waiting for a bus.

Then, at five o'clock, the day running out, William's patience running out, my right arm running out, I finally caught one. It weighed maybe six pounds and jumped higher than my head before coming to the boat.

As William—really smiling now—shipped the pole and got ready to start the engine for the run back to the lodge, I said, "William, I've decided that I am not going to give you a tip this week."

William, always open for comedy, said, "Oh really? No tip?"

"No," I said. "Instead, I'm calling Pope Francis and asking him to make you a saint."

William smiled slyly. "Oh, that's too much. A small tip would be enough. Really."

Will and I cracked up. We still had four more days of fishing with this smart and funny guide in one of the fishiest and most beautiful places we'd ever been.

Spirits were high back at the lodge that night. Rum drinks flowed. We celebrated my first permit, first tarpon, first snook, my grand slam. We celebrated the great guides, the fabulous Cuban sunshine, and the endless fish-filled flats of Cayo Largo. Oh, yeah, and the end of old Cold War enmities between our two countries.

A friendly Cuban permit had extended a warm welcome to his former enemy, an American. One week later, President Obama met with Raoul Castro, laughing and shaking hands like old pals.

Coincidence? I don't think so.

Chapter 18

The Angler in Winter

HOW DID IT COME TO THIS?

That is a question anyone might ask about himself six decades into life. Actually, at virtually *any* time after consciousness kicks in, though it usually takes a while to get around to it. Why is this particular kind of person staring back at me from the mirror, instead of some other? In my case, why an aching retired construction worker turned writer and college teacher? And most of all, why a fisherman? Why not a football fan, a golfer, a theater enthusiast, a marathon runner? Why do I continue to spend so much of my very limited time here on this planet throwing hooks at fish?

It's not like angling is a family tradition. My grandfathers certainly did not fish. America may have been the land of opportunity for people of that generation coming from the Old World, but that mostly meant *the opportunity to work*. And that's what my grandfathers did. All their lives. To them, hobbies, avocations, or "interests" were alien notions. Their only interest was supporting their families.

Even the second generation working class Americans like my father were not wholly enamored with effete hobbies like sport fishing. I remember that, when I was in grade school, there were a couple old hexagonal steel casting rods standing in the corner of our garage among pieces of pipe and lumber. So, it's possible he fished before World War II, when he was a teenager, but I'm not sure. I don't recall ever hearing him speak of it, and I remember almost everything any grown man had to say about fishing when I was a kid. I do know that when my father returned from Europe at the end of the war he married my mother—his high school sweetheart—and set to work, like his father before him.

He spent the next thirty-five years or so working as the shipping manager at Great Lakes Carbon Co. in the dusty industrial city of Niagara Falls, New York. He also played accordion at Italian and Polish-American weddings on weekends to feed what would eventually be seven of us children. Again, like his father before him, he had no chance to pursue leisure time activities. There was no leisure time. He did not fish.

And yet, somehow, by the time I was eight years old, I was already a fanatic. While on a family vacation in the Finger Lakes that summer (there were only three of us kids then), I harangued my folks into buying me a fiberglass casting rod and an Ocean City level wind reel—now long gone to wherever old fishing tackle ends up. What has survived is a photo of me dated 1956 in which I'm holding the rod in one hand, and a rope stringer in the other; dangling from it is what appears to be a mooneye, a small trash fish of the sort I spent the rest of my childhood pursuing. I've been fishing ever since.

Three days ago, I spent several hours at the mouth of the Anchor River near my home here in Southcentral Alaska, hurling heavy Clouser Minnows into the surf of Cook Inlet against a ferocious onshore wind. Then I came home and ate four Advils, my neck and shoulder aching. The next day I got up early and drove one hundred twenty miles to the confluence of the Kenai and Russian Rivers to meet my old fishing partner, Will Rice. Wadered up, we marched for two miles uphill on a well-maintained trail, clambered down a near vertical, boulder-strewn ravine into the Russian River canyon, and fished our way downstream—stumbling on a murderous jumble of slippery, pyramid-shaped rocks underfoot much of the way. Late in the afternoon, we dragged our sorry keisters back up to the parking lot. Between the two of us, we have attached into our skeletons enough titanium to build a mountain bike. Without the surgeries, neither one of us would be wading trout streams today—let alone one as wicked as the Russian.

When I opened the door of my truck, the soft cervical collar I wore on the drive from home rolled out onto the gravel. Will and I traded glances, each hoping the other had enough range of motion to actually bend over and pick the thing up. Will—who fishes wearing a back pack with a half a ton of camera equipment inside—somehow managed to hang onto the door handle and crouch just far enough to snatch the neck brace off the ground with two fingertips. There was a certain amount of groaning involved. Subsequently, there was also a certain amount of beer involved.

Arriving home—a three-hour drive, thanks to the Alaska Department of Transportation's ever-diligent road maintenance—I could barely swing my legs out of the truck cab. I considered sleeping out there in the driveway that night, but this is a small town and I didn't want rumors to start about my marriage. I managed to make it to the house. This time, the post-fishing self-medication required not only the usual ibuprofen, but also a couple muscle relaxants and more vodka than I'd admit to my doctor. (Don't try this at home.) Later, feeling surprisingly well again, I made plans to meet another pal at the Anchor River this morning. Which I did.

Recently some wiseacre asked me, "Would you rather fish or fornicate?" (Ok, that wasn't the particular word used, but you know that.) I answered as honestly as I could: "Well, at my age, I can still fish for hours on end without resting. In fact, I can still fish several times the same day like that."

All of which is to say that I'm not dead yet, but I am also not the boy in that photo anymore, not by a long shot. Not that I'm complaining. Well, I *am* complaining about the physical aches and pains and the fact that I used to be able to do exciting and pleasurable things all day long—like casting into the wind or wading difficult rivers—without meds.

Still, there are also some benefits to being one of the greybeards on a river now. Don't get me wrong: I'm not claiming to possess the legendary wisdom that's supposed to come with age—I'm still waiting for that to kick in—but, one of the blessings that actually does arrive is freedom from the slavery of deceit, or at least the option to choose a more factual telling of a day's fishing efforts at every opportunity. Meaning only that there comes a point at which you just don't care if others know that you caught nothing but little fish that day, or nothing but trash fish, or nothing but really little really trashy fish. Or simply nothing.

It was not always this way. I will be the first to admit I may have reshaped the facts of a fishing trip or two into a form that presented my modest talents with rod and reel under generously favorable light. But, brother, I've seen a hell of a lot worse big fat liars over the years.

LIAR, LIAR, PANTS ON FIRE, NOSE IS LONGER THAN . . . ETC.

In 1982, when my wife Lin and I moved to Alaska, I took her fishing for the first time in her life. Somehow she had never sampled the joys of trying to outwit scaly, coldblooded creatures with marble-sized brains before the day we went fishing for cohos in a small river just south of Anchorage.

Lin's first fish *ever* was a silver salmon that must have weighed ten pounds. She also caught two others nearly as large. To put that in perspective, in the first ten years I fished, all the fish I caught, *in toto*, would not have come close to the combined weight of the three salmon she landed her first day. Was she elated? Converted? "Hooked for life," as the cliché goes? Not quite. She fished exactly twice more after that: one lovely afternoon on a Kodiak Island stream catching small Dolly Varden char on dry flies, and another catching grayling and lake trout in the foothills of the Alaska Range. And then she hung up the tackle and quit. Forever. The whole undertaking—selecting the perfect fly, making the best cast, fooling the fish—simply left her unmoved. Whatever virus it was that made me certifiably mad for the sport did not infect her brain.

To this day she loves to go fishing with me, loves to be on the water, but has no desire to catch fish herself. None. For some reason, she apparently does not feel that her self-worth is tied to her skill at catching fish. (Women are incomprehensible.) Which means, of course, she has no reason to lie about catching fish, and therefore cannot imagine why anyone else would blatantly massacre the truth the way we fishermen do.

Her first contact with what I've come to understand is Normal Angler Bullshit (NAB) came as a shock to her. Another weekend in that first year in Alaska we drove south two hundred miles from Anchorage to the Anchor River so I could fish for steelhead. Lin was in grad school and planned to study while I fished. Being steelhead season, the weather was gray, cold, and rainy. No problem for Lin; it would not be the last time she happily sat in the warm, dry truck reading while I stood in a river in the rain.

But there is rain and there is rain. We drove down the Kenai Peninsula through a constant deluge that Friday afternoon. Every river we crossed was high and muddy and still rising. And the Anchor is the longest of them, with the most tributaries, draining a huge area of soggy tundra in the Caribou Hills. When we crossed the bridge near the hotel, the river was raging, standing waves the color of lentil soup sloshing over the banks, water running through the Bridge Hole parking lot. Uprooted cottonwood trees tumbled downstream. Cutbanks calved clods of earth into the flood. No one could fish it, of course. No one would try. Not even me.

I spent the weekend in the bar of the Anchor River Inn pretending to watch what I think may have been the World Series, but really eyeing the rain slashing at the windows—hoping, as only a fisherman might, that somehow it was going to abate and the river would drop enough to fish. It was still raining as we gave up and headed north for Anchorage on Sunday.

On Monday, Lin stopped by the job I was working on—I was a commercial wallcovering contractor in Anchorage for nearly thirty years—a new office building. I was hanging vinyl wallpaper in the hallways. One of the new tenants, an insurance representative, was moving into his office. I heard him hammering on the walls and peeked in to find him hanging framed photos of himself gripping trout and salmon. I struck up a conversation with him. Lin stopped by and walked in just in time to hear the guy tell me he'd caught twenty steelhead over the weekend. Guess where . . .

Bingo. The Anchor River.

Lin's chin dropped. She started sputtering. I rushed her out into the hallway before she could say it. "He's lying! We were there. Nobody could fish in that mess, could they?"

I agreed that she was right on both counts: Nobody could fish that mess, and yes, he was lying.

"But why would anybody do that?" she asked, astounded.

I tried to explain the concept of Normal Angler Bullshit. But she would never understand that if you aren't catching anything, you crave just one fish. If you're catching some fish, you want to catch more, lots more. If you are catching lots of fish, you want to catch bigger fish. How could I explain to her that if you've had a great day of fishing, the only thing that makes it better is telling someone how good it was. And, most importantly, that if the fishing has been abysmal, the same response is called for: telling someone how good it was.

Lin has spent the past thirty-five years with me, and still has never fully come to accept the concept of NAB. Probably never will.

Not because she's a woman. Because she doesn't fish.

IN PRAISE OF PLUNKING

Another benefit of running on well-worn tires (I hesitate to use the word "bald" at my age) is that not only do you not care how few fish you catch anymore, you also don't care that it's mostly your own fault. As is true in poker, the reason some fishermen catch far more fish than others is unrelated to luck. They are simply much, much better at it. I'm not one of those guys. And I don't care.

Many fishing skills are so subtle they are nearly impossible to discern in an angler: expertly reading a river for lies and holding water, making pinpoint assessments of what the fish are feeding on and then selecting the perfect size and shaped imitation, knowing the hour of the day or stage of the tide that will best produce fish, the ability to sense almost imperceptible strikes. Those are things you just can't measure, or even see, most of the time. But casting? Good casting is a beautiful thing. And there is just no way to disguise bad casting. Take mine, for example.

Consider my every collapsed cast falling short of cruising permit; my every out of control cast landing on top of spooky, midge-sipping rainbows; my constant tailing loops and casting knots; every hat snagged by a low flying hook, every pair of sunglasses launched off my head, every fly stuck past the barb in the back of my vest or waders—or my neck or ear. I cannot hide my bad casting. And I don't care anymore.

Twenty years ago, on my first flats fishing trip ever, I drove our Mexican guide, Agustin, insane. He is rather notorious among

Ascension Bay anglers for having a generally dour countenance and an extremely short temper. He's a really grumpy, but knowledgeable, guide. Toward the end of our stay at Casa Blanca Lodge, I was up on the casting deck when a permit showed up dead ahead. Excited into that state of manic stumblebumery that only a cruising permit can elicit, I forgot to wait for Agustin to jam the pole in the sand and turn the boat. My backcast wrapped around his legs. My forecast nearly hauled him off the platform. Needless to say the permit left the scene laughing.

Agustin was not laughing. "Señor," he said, "that was the most worst cast of the whole week."

I felt pretty bad about ruining a permit shot like that. Not just for myself. I had been doing it all week, and the poor guy was exceedingly frustrated. Guides are as intent on successful fishing days as we sports are, for their own reasons. It's what they do; their reputations are at stake. With an incompetent neophyte flats fisherman like me in the boat, Agustin could see his yearly tally of landed fish was not getting any help this week.

Finally, more weary than angry, he said, "I'm the head guide here. I get to choose which guests I guide with each week. I picked you guys because you are from Alaska. I thought you could cast very far into the wind."

And that was Agustin's mistake.

In saltwater, long casts are essential. Flats fish are cruising, hunting prey. They never stop moving, and you have to deliver a fly to them before they either swim out of range, or see the boat and flee. The farther you can cast, the better your chances. On the ocean flats off Cuba, our guide—from his high vantage point up on the poling platform—would spot permit when they were a hundred yards out. He would stop the boat, turn it so that we could cast off the port side (being right-handed), and hold the boat in place. When he could see that the permit were within casting range, he would say something like, "Cast, nine-o'clock, twenty meters."

That's about a sixty-foot cast, which does not sound like much. But on my home river, the Anchor, a sixty-foot cast would put the fly about thirty feet into the woods on the other side of the river. And so I get very little practice throwing that much line. We simply don't cast very far here in Southcentral Alaska. In fact, much of the time, on the Kenai Peninsula streams that I mostly fish, we don't cast at all. We plunk.

On the road system of the peninsula, the premier blue ribbon trout stream is the Russian River, which is no wider than the Anchor in most places. Plus, it flows through a heavily wooded canyon—meaning that even if you stood in the very middle of the river, you could not put sixty feet of fly line in the air without snagging the trees either in front of you or behind you. On top of that, most of our trout fishing is nymphing with strike indicators, which requires constant mending. Meaning what you do not want is a lot of flyline on the water creating drag.

On my beloved Anchor River, we fish primarily for silver salmon or steelhead. Again, it's plunking. Even when fishing Clouser Minnows in the saltchuck for salmon, the fish are generally less than thirty feet away from whichever bank you are standing on. It's also "combat" fishing when the run is on, with guys lining both banks on the tide change, and walking up and down behind you at any given moment: not good conditions for practicing your double haul. The crowds are much thinner during steelhead season, but once again it's almost all Glo Bug fishing—which is basically nymph fishing with a hunk of yarn instead of an imitation insect. Realistically, even if you decided to reach out with a longer cast for some reason, the last thing you'd want is a nice tight loop when you have a strike indicator, two split shots, and a fly boloing through the air.

Yes, there are wider rivers to fish. The Kenai is a quarter mile across in places. But, again, you do not want miles of line out in the heavy glacial current. And once again the angling *mode du jour* is plunking with strike indicators and egg imitations (mostly the infernal pegged beads, but don't get me started).

Bottom line, so to speak, is that when you've spent three decades or so lobbing split shots and bobber rigs into streams that are three rod lengths across, you are simply not going to develop tournament-worthy casting chops. Muscle memory being what it is, even preparing for spring bonefish trips by spending much of February and March each year now practicing casting on the frozen lawn of the nearby Ocean Shores Motel, my skill set has improved only marginally since that first trip to Ascension Bay. Let's just say that Agustin would not be a lot happier with me today than he was back then.

All of this raises the question of whether I would cast any better even if I actually knew how to, once a permit or tarpon shows up. All winter, in preparation for a spring flats fishing trip, I watch the casting instruction videos on YouTube: "Improve Your Double Haul," "Casting Into the Wind," "Eliminate Tailing Loops!" And then I go stand on the lawn behind the Ocean Shores Motel. On my best days I will have a run of tight loops and strong casts. The rod will load as if the line weighs a couple tons. The leader will unfurl as straight as a laser—even into the wind off Kachemak Bay—and I will set the bright pink hookless fly out there on the grass, so far away that I let it lie there and walk to it, using the rod tip to measure nine-foot increments across the snow or frozen grass. Seventy-five feet! Even ninety, once in a while. My heart swells with self-satisfaction. I am going to kick saltwater fish butts.

The weeks go by and I lie in bed at night imagining the power-cast I am going to unleash when the first permit shows itself. I can already feel the tension in the loaded rod as it comes forward from the back cast, see the flyline hurling through the rod guides, rocketing out above the glittering water, the fly landing seventy feet out there, eighty, ninety. The guide saying, "Perfect."

Then I'm up on the casting desk for real, my hard-earned confidence buoying me. All those frozen fingers I suffered practicing in the snow is finally paying off. The guide counts down the approach of whatever fish he can see from up there on the platform: "Forty meters. Thirty meters."

I squint at the inscrutable surface, seeing nothing but the sun, and the scudding clouds moving across it. But I'm ready.

"Get ready," the guide says. "Twenty meters. Cast!"

And then I see the permit. For some reason, my backcast seems to hit a wall of solid air behind me and stalls. I slash the rod forward and feel nothing. Two more ineffectual false casts, the line as limp as over boiled linguini. The fish are only thirty *feet* away now. Three rod lengths. Even I can cast thirty feet. And I do, finally.

"Strip! Strip!" the guide says.

Out of the corner of my eye, I can see him crouching to keep this profile low.

When I manage to get all the slack out of the line and strip the big mantis shrimp fly, the permit—six or eight of them—all turn and chase it. But they are too close. They see the boat and veer off, crisscrossing each other in their panic as they vanish. The guide just shakes his head. He is much more affable than old Agustin. But he cannot hide his disappointment.

Yes, I'm sorry I blew that chance. Am I ever going to be a great flats fisherman? I'd say thc chances are about the same as me becoming an astronaut or a pro golfer. Am I ashamed of my casting? A little I suppose. But, really—unlike most things these days—it's just not as painful as it used to be.

THE CHOSEN

In my long life, I've had the good fortune to fish to some of the best angling destinations in the world. I mean, for a guy who spent the first thirty-two years of his life wading the fetid industrial waters of Western New York, I've been blessed in the second thirty-two years. Living in Alaska helped, of course.

In 1985 (God, thirty years ago now!), my brother Marty and I decided to fish a wild and remote river in the Bristol Bay drainage of western Alaska. I'd seen an article in a fly-fishing magazine about the "best rainbow trout river in North America." The photos of monster trout caught on deer hair mouse flies leapt off the pages at us. The author of the piece would not name the river. He pseudonymously referred to it only as The Chosen. The implication being that if you got to fish that river, God had selected you as one of his faves. He also happened to mention floating down to the Yupik village of Quinhagak. There are not a lot of rivers flowing through Quinhagak. The actual number is one.

With our gear and a river raft, we flew commercial jet service to the regional hub of Bethel and then caught a float plane out to Kagati Lake in the Ahklun Mountains. The now legendary Kanektok flows about seventy-five miles southwest from the lake to the Bering Sea. To this day, it is considered one of the best rivers in the world.

It was the worst fishing trip of my life. I was depressed for months afterward.

Not that anyone had misstated the quality of the fishing there; it may indeed be excellent. I wouldn't know. We could not fish for the first fifty miles or so of the float trip. The river was in flood stage, an enormous chocolate milkshake spilling across the tundra. It was so high we couldn't even find the main channel in places. Braids took us into dense willow stands; at one point we had to saw our way out, the raft jammed against an impenetrable thicket. And it rained all day, every day.

With all the gravel bars submerged, dry campsites were nearly impossible to find. The subarctic wind howled across the bleak gray landscape, incessantly. And it rained some more. The fish were impossible to locate in the massive flood.

In the last two or three days, the rain stopped and the water dropped enough to fish—and we caught some nice trout and bright fresh chum salmon. But, even the better fishing and the warm sun could not brighten the muddy, flood-blighted river basin in my mind. The point had been made: We were not among those chosen by God to experience the "best trout fishing in North America." It was like arriving in the biblical promised land of milk and honey to find that the milk had gone sour, and the honey was infested with ants.

All of that is ridiculous, of course. The real trouble was that I had allowed myself to actually believe in the idea of being so special that I deserved—for reasons I can't fathom—to be delivered into secret heavenly fishing that others would never know. Thirty years later, those kinds of delusions have thankfully shrunken up and vanished like a drying river slough. Have I had some extraordinary trips? Yes indeed. But I just don't need to see them as exclusive or special, or God forbid, privileged experiences. And I certainly have no desire to be in on the secret. Like the Normal Angler Bullshit, and the shame of bad casting, I'm too old for that now. Maybe a teensy bit of that legendary wisdom is beginning to trickle in at last.